Exploring Liberal Arts in the 21st Century

Japan Association of International Liberal Arts
日本国際教養学会

写真提供
Aflo
iStock

音声ファイルのダウンロード/ストリーミング

CD マーク表示がある箇所は、音声を弊社 HP より無料でダウンロード／ストリーミングすることができます。下記 URL の書籍詳細ページに音声ダウンロードアイコンがございますのでそちらから自習用音声としてご活用ください。

https://www.seibido.co.jp/ad723

Exploring Liberal Arts in the 21st Century

Copyright ©2025 by Japan Association of International Liberal Arts

*All rights reserved for Japan.
No part of this book may be reproduced in any form
without permission from Seibido Co., Ltd.*

はしがき

　グローバル化が加速する現在, 国際共通語としての英語の重要性は益々高まりつつあります。英語教育は今, 世の中の期待に応えることができるよう, 改善を続けることが求められています。では, 大学の共通教育で提供される英語はどうあるべきでしょうか。本書は, 日本国際教養学会英語教材プロジェクトチーム (以下, プロジェクトチーム) のこの問いに対する回答を具体的に示したものです。

　英語をツールとして使用する能力が重視されていますが, 大学で求められている英語教育は, いわゆる, 「英会話」レベルの内容ではありません。自分の趣味, 週末の出来事, 長期休暇の予定等について互いに伝え合うような活動の意義を否定するつもりはありません。身近な題材について英語で伝え合うことによって, 大学生の「英語でコミュニケーションを取ろうとする意欲」(Willingness to Communicate) を高めることができれば, それは素晴らしいことです。しかし大学は本来学問を学ぶ学術的な場であり, そこで提供される英語も知的好奇心を刺激し教養を高めるものであるべきです。

　例えば, 2010年に日本学術会議より文部科学省に手交された『大学教育における分野別質保証の在り方について』では, 大学学士課程で提供されるべき英語教育は, アカデミック・リーディング, アカデミック・ライティングそしてプレゼンテーションを核とした「英語によるリテラシー教育」となっています。これを英語教材として具現化するためには, まず認知負荷の高い読み応えのある英語のパッセージが必要となります。大学生の知的好奇心を満たす知的な内容でなければなりません。しかも共通教育で使用するためには, 特定の学問領域だけでなく, 様々な分野を包括的に扱うことが求められます。

　本書の各ユニットに掲載されているパッセージの多くは, 多様な分野で研究を行っているプロジェクトチームのメンバーがその専門性を活かして書き下ろしたものです。大学における学び, 先端工学, 哲学, 社会学, 学際的研究等, その内容は多岐にわたっています。読んで理解して終わりではなく, 理解した内容に基づいて各自で深く考えることを意図して書かれたパッセージです。単なる読解教材としてではなく, 自分の思考を英語で伝える能力を育成し, さらには専門教育への「橋渡し」をも想定した内容・構成となっています。

　なお, 本書の英文につきましては, David Chart氏, Mark Taylor氏, Douglas Parkin氏そしてBill Benfield氏に最終確認をしていただきました。また, 本書を出版するに当たり, 成美堂の中澤ひろ子氏には, その企画から編集まですべてにわたりお世話をいただきました。心よりお礼を申し上げます。

日本国際教養学会英語教材プロジェクトチーム

Preface

As globalization accelerates, English as a world language has become much more important than ever before. More and more people wish to be good speakers of English, and researchers and teachers in Japan have been working hard to make their wishes come true. So what should English education at university be like? JAILA has been working on this problem since its establishment, and this book is one of our attempts to address it.

First of all, English is a tool for global communication, and the value of the language in that sense cannot be denied. Indeed, exercises oriented towards this goal, such as greetings, talking about your hobbies, giving directions, etc., will help improve your willingness to communicate. On the other hand, a university is an academic institution where you enrich your education, and what you learn there should stimulate your intellectual curiosity. To meet this goal, English teaching materials should be substantial and comprehensive.

Most of the reading passages in this book were specially written for this project by team members with remarkable academic accomplishments in their own specialized fields. The topics include university education, advanced engineering, philosophy, sociology, literature, and interdisciplinary studies. In other words, you can learn the essentials of different fields of research and study in English. Working as a bridge between general and technical education, this book will encourage you to read and think deeply about each topic through:

- a variety of high-interest warm-up and comprehension exercises, and
- further studies giving practice in writing, speaking, and thinking in English.

Finally, we wish to thank David Chart, Mark Taylor, Douglas Parkin, and Bill Benfield for their unstinting guidance on idiomatic English usage. We would also like to thank Hiroko Nakazawa at SEIBIDO for her valuable and persistent advice. Without their cooperation and kindness, this book could never have been published.

ELT Project Team at the Japan Association of International Liberal Arts

執筆者一覧 （監修：那須 雅子・吉田 安曇・岩中 貴裕）

Unit	タイトル	執筆担当者
1	Explore the World Beyond the Syllabus	深谷 素子
2	The University and Civic Engagement: A Brief History	草薙 優加
3	Life Design for Centenarians	佐藤 宏子・寺西 雅之・吉田 安曇
4	Can Humans Really Fall in Love with Robots?	原口 治
5	Business in Asia: Global Talents in Japan	那須 雅子
6	What Literary Works Teach Us	久世 恭子
7	Advice from the Philosopher Nietzsche: Have a Strong Will to Live Well	宮上 久仁子
8	Three Tools for Learning at University	岩中 貴裕
9	Laugh and Then Think: The Ig Nobel Prize	北 和丈
10	Ecological Thinking	竹下 浩子・吉田 安曇
11	Healthcare, and Quality of Life in Two Cities	内山 八郎
12	Sports, Culture, and Communication	Mark Sheehan
13	Form and Function in Classical Music	Edward Sarich
14	Looking at Art of Other Cultures	五十嵐 潤美
15	Interdisciplinary Studies: Where Science and Humanities Meet	寺西 雅之・吉田 安曇
p.8	プロセスライティング―プロセスを踏んで書こう―	五十嵐 潤美・ウィックストラム 由有夏

本書の構成

各ユニットの構成は，基本的に以下のようになっています。

Warm-up

本文を読む際に必要となる背景的知識を活性化するための質問です。英語での表現活動に慣れていない学生のために Useful Expressions/Useful Words and Phrases を載せています。ペア，または小グループで英語を用いて意見交換をすることを想定した構成になっています。

Pre-reading Vocabulary Check

本文中で使用されている重要な語を確認するための活動です。大学1年生にはかなり難しい語も含まれています。英英辞典を積極的に活用しましょう。難易度の高い語を平易な英語で表現する能力の育成を図ることも目的としています。

Reading

日本国際教養学会英語教材プロジェクトチームのメンバーが各自の専門性を活かして作成した passage です。「英語力」の向上と同時に「思考力」の向上をもたらすことを目標とし，各専門領域の橋渡しとなる内容となっています。多様な専門分野のトピックについて英語で読み，大学生としての国際教養を身に付けましょう。

True or False

本文の内容理解を確認するための活動です。本文のどの部分に基づいて判断したのかを考えさせることによって，内容に対する深い理解がもたらされます。False と判断した場合は，その理由を明確にすることによって，分析的思考力の育成を図ることを目的としています。

Comprehension Questions

本文の内容理解をさらに深めるための活動です。本文に基づいて自分の英語で答えることによって，内容に対する深い理解をもたらし，英語による表現力を伸ばすことを目的としています。

Summary

本文の概要を思い出しながら，本文中で使用されていた重要語の定着を図ることを目的としています。各語の最初のアルファベットをヒントとして提示しています。解答の確認は音声を聞いて行います。

Discussion & Writing

本文に対する理解を深めた後で自分の考えを表現するための活動です。英語で Discussion を行い，さらにその内容についてライティングでまとめましょう。まずは「パラグラフの構成と種類」について p.VII で確認し，「パラグラフライティングのプロセス」について p.VIII で学びましょう。尚，「エッセイの構成」については，p.IX にまとめています。

パラグラフの構成と種類を確認しよう

●パラグラフの構成

Topic Sentence	パラグラフの main idea について書く
Supporting Sentence(s)	Topic Sentence に対する理由・裏付け・具体例・補足など
Concluding Sentence	パラグラフのまとめ

●パラグラフの種類

Description	特定のものを描写する。一番重要なものを先に書き、細かいことを後に述べる。
Cause/Effect	ある物事がなぜ、どのようにして起こったのか、その原因と結果について述べる。
Compare/Contrast	2つ以上の物事の似た部分と違う部分をそれぞれ比較対照して述べていく。
Opinion	ある事柄に対する賛否など、自分の意見を述べる。

プロセス・ライティング—プロセスを踏んで書こう—

英文エッセイを書く際には、下記のようなプロセスに沿って仕上げます。

1. ブレインストーム

➢ トピックを選ぶ

アイデアを集める：トピックについて自由にアイデアや発想されたものを書き出す。ブレインストームの方法には、(1) 箇条書きでワードやフレーズを書き出す<u>リスト</u>、(2) 自由に文章を書いていく<u>フリーライティング</u>、(3) マップでアイデアをつなげて書き出す<u>マインドマッピング</u>などがある。

➢ 整理する：情報を整理し、アイデアをまとめる。

2. アウトライン

★アウトラインとは、エッセイに入れる情報のリストをさします。

➢ エッセイの主題文を最初に書く
➢ それぞれの段落のエッセイの構成を示す
➢ 議論するアイデアの内容をエッセイに書く順番通りに記す

エッセイを書き始める前にアウトラインを書くことで、エッセイの構成が整然と明確に整い、重要なポイントが抜け落ちるのを防ぐことができます。

3. 書き始め

➢ エッセイを、2. で作成したアウトラインに沿って最後まで書く

4. 編集

➢ 構成と内容をよく見直し改訂する
➢ 情報を加える箇所、または不必要だと思われる箇所を見つけ修正する
➢ 他の人に読んでもらい意見を聞く
➢ 校正：スペルや文法に間違いなどないか確認する
➢ 最後の修正をする

5. 最終稿

➢ 内容のほかフォーマットや必要事項なども最後にもう一度確認し、最終稿を完成させる

The Basic Structure of an Essay

英文エッセイは、通常三つの基本部分から構成されます。

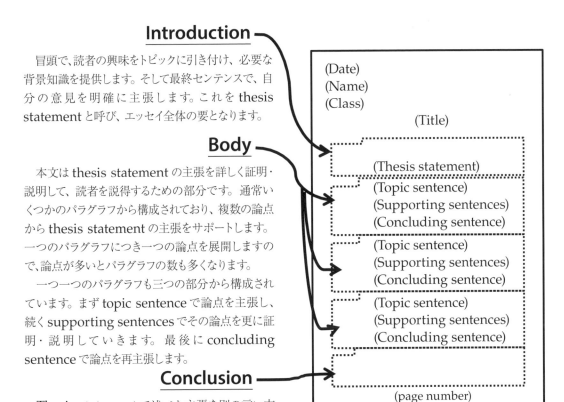

Introduction

冒頭で、読者の興味をトピックに引き付け、必要な背景知識を提供します。そして最終センテンスで、自分の意見を明確に主張します。これを thesis statement と呼び、エッセイ全体の要となります。

Body

本文は thesis statement の主張を詳しく証明・説明して、読者を説得するための部分です。通常いくつかのパラグラフから構成されており、複数の論点から thesis statement の主張をサポートします。一つのパラグラフにつき一つの論点を展開しますので、論点が多いとパラグラフの数も多くなります。

一つ一つのパラグラフも三つの部分から構成されています。まず topic sentence で論点を主張し、続く supporting sentences でその論点を更に証明・説明していきます。最後に concluding sentence で論点を再主張します。

Conclusion

Thesis statement で述べた主張を別の言い方でもう一度述べるか、本文の論点を要約します。

References

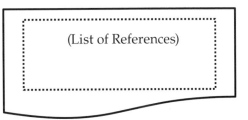

もし本文の中で、他の人が書いたものを引用した場合、必ずそのことを明示しなければなりません。引用したものは、本文の中に示すと同時に、巻末にリストを付け加えます。

＊専門分野による書き方の違い＊

上記に示したのは基本的な英文アカデミックエッセイの書き方です。専門的なリサーチペーパーを書くときは、分野によって構成や引用のスタイルが異なります。よく使われるのは文学系の MLA、心理学・社会学系の APA、歴史系の Chicago、理系の IMRAD などです。リサーチペーパーの書き方を学ぶときに、先生におたずねください。

CONTENTS

Unit 01　Explore the World Beyond the Syllabus ……………………………… 12
分野：大学での学びについての総論
概要：内田樹氏の著書『街場の教育論』、第3講「キャンパスとメンター」の概要を英訳し、解説したユニット。講義要項を見て講義をカタログショッピングするような学習観に真っ向から反論する内田氏は、カオスとしてのキャンパスで「すでにはじまっているゲームに巻き込まれる」体験、そこで「自分には理解できない『高み』にいる」メンターに呼び寄せられ、自分の限界を乗り越える体験こそが大学での学びであると説く。内田氏の熱い持論について英語で読んで考えてみよう。

Unit 02　The University and Civic Engagement: A Brief History ………………… 20
分野：本書で扱う学術分野に関する説明
概要：世界の東西を問わず、大学の学部は人文学、社会科学、自然科学、応用科学のいずれか、あるいは分野横断型の学際研究分野を基盤に設置されている。本ユニットでは、専攻分野に偏重しがちな視野を拡げるため、まず、自身の専攻が諸研究分野のどこに位置して何を目指しているのか、他の分野とどのような関係性があるのかを理解し専攻分野を越えた統合的な教養を得る手がかりを探ってみよう。

Unit 03　Life Design for Centenarians ……………………………………………… 28
分野：社会学
概要：日本は1970年に国連の定める「高齢化社会」を迎え、わずか35年後の2005年には世界で一番の高齢社会となった。明治期・大正期には国民の平均寿命が40代前半だった日本が、21世紀には世界有数の長寿国となったのである。本ユニットでは、このような高水準かつ急激なスピードで進む日本の高齢化の特徴、寿命の延長と高齢者の若返り、活動的な高齢者の増加等について理解を深め、人生100年を想定した人生設計の必要性について学ぼう。

Unit 04　Can Humans Really Fall in Love with Robots? ………………………… 36
分野：先端工学
概要：昨今話題の最年少棋士藤井聡太四段にも影響を与えたと言われている「人工知能（Artificial Intelligence）」。本章では、「人間と人工知能ロボットとの恋愛関係が未来では可能となるのか」という刺激的なテーマを提示する。「人間と技術」の関係を、二項対立を超越した視点で捉え、人間の存在意義を問うコミュニケーションの在り方を、身近なレベルで考えてみよう。

Unit 05　Business in Asia: Global Talents in Japan ……………………………… 44
分野：国際ビジネス
概要：グローバル社会の中で、日本的なモノを輸出しようとする企業が増加している。日本で拡大した野菜スイーツ事業をアジア太平洋地域に展開するビジネスマンのインタビューをもとに、日本と海外を行き来するグローバル人材に必要な「教養」とは何かについて考えよう。

Unit 06　What Literary Works Teach Us ……………………………………………… 52
分野：文学
概要：文学作品では、しばしば、出来事や登場人物等に関する解釈がいくつか存在する。本ユニットでは、戯曲 *Pygmalion* に注目し、ロンドン初演の2年後に作者が ending を書き換えて、さらに sequel を追加したという事実から、文学は読み手や演じ手によって様々に解釈される可能性を持つことを学ぼう。同時に、文学作品は、外国語学習においても言語、文化、人間形成等の点から重要な意味を持つことを理解しよう。

Unit 07　Advice from the Philosopher Nietzsche: Have a Strong Will to Live Well …… 60
分野：哲学
概要：ニーチェの「悲劇の誕生」をもとに、現代社会が抱える「生きにくさ」を考える。ニーチェによると、古代ギリシア悲劇は、ふとしたことから苦しい人生を歩むことになろうとも、それも自然な人間の定めとの理解を促し、人々を慰めていた。それが精神的支えとなり、人は自分を受け入れ、過酷な運命を乗り越えようとの勇気を得ていたという。ニーチェが自分を生きようとする人々に与えている忠告を現在の文脈で考えてみよう。

Unit 08　Three Tools for Learning at University 68
分野：社会人基礎力
概要：所属する学部に関係なく学士課程のすべての学生が習得することが求められている資質が「社会人基礎力」である。これは「前に踏み出す力」、「考え抜く力」、「チーム働く力」という3つの能力で構成されており、「職場や地域社会で多様な人々と仕事をしていくために必要な基礎的な力」とされている。どのような姿勢で日々の大学生活を送るべきかについて理解を深めよう。

Unit 09　Laugh and Then Think: The Ig Nobel Prize 76
分野：科学
概要：かのノーベル賞のパロディとも言われ、近年では日本からの受賞者の多さでも注目を集めている「イグ・ノーベル賞」。創設以来の数十年でその栄誉（？）に浴してきた突飛で滑稽な研究の数々には失笑を禁じ得ないが、その詳細を知れば知るほど、笑って済ませるには勿体ない知の輝きが見えてくる。この賞の存在意義を考えることによって、科学の本質にナナメ上から切り込もう。

Unit 10　Ecological Thinking 84
分野：環境
概要：エコバッグ、エコカー、エコブーム等に代表されるように、「エコ」という言葉は、環境にやさしいという意味を連想させる。そもそも、「エコ」のもとになっているエコロジー（ecology）は、生態系という意味があり、環境へのやさしさを考える場合には他の生物との共存が必要である。そこで、本当の意味で「エコ」な生き方とは何かについて、過去に起きた生態系の事例から考えよう。

Unit 11　Healthcare and Quality of Life in Two Cities 92
分野：国際保健学
概要：現代人、特に日本人の平均寿命を始めとする健康指標は、非常に高い健康水準を示しているが、世界、特にアフリカのサブサハラ地域に目を向けると、歴然として存在する健康格差が浮き彫りになる。この章では世界保健機関による、日本の熊本市で生活する一人の女性とシエラ・レオーネ共和国のフリータウンに生きる一人の女性の物語を基に、経済や医療保健システムが個人の人生や生活の質にどのように影響を与え得るのかを考えよう。

Unit 12　Sports, Culture, and Communication 100
分野：スポーツ
概要：本ユニットでは国際交流と文化交流を促進するためのスポーツの役割に注目する。各国で行われている国際的なスポーツイベントにおいて、アスリートは様々な人々に出会い、様々な文化交流を行う。スポーツは文化交流を促進するために非常に有効なメソッドと言える。なぜならアスリートは、国境を越えてスポーツマンシップに基づき、スポーツという共通の題材について対話することができるからである。国際言語であると同時に、多文化理解を育み、世界平和に貢献する役割を持つスポーツの意義について考えよう。

Unit 13　Form and Function in Classical Music 108
分野：音楽史
概要：本ユニットでは、1600年から1750年のバロック時代の発展に影響を与えた歴史要因に焦点を当てる。30年戦争が終わった1648年には、フランスはヨーロッパにおいて支配的な権力を持つようになった。ルイ14世は、彼の72年の生涯を通して、芸術に関して寛大な後援者であり続けた。指揮者・室内楽・オペラ・フーガ等の複雑な音楽作品の発展を含め、今日も使用されているさまざまな音楽の構造や形式の革新を掌握したバロック時代について学ぼう。

Unit 14　Looking at Art of Other Cultures 116
分野：美術史
概要：芸術は国境を超えると言われるが、それは必ずしも正しくない。他文化の芸術を見る我々の眼は無垢で中立的ものではなく、必ず自らの属する文化、時の政治状況や信条によって影響を受けざるを得ない。他者に対するその眼差しは時に文化間の衝突を招く。顕著な例として、植民地時代の南アジア美術と西洋がそれらをどのように評価したかについて学び、観察者の主観とその感性の危うさについて考えよう。

Unit 15　Interdisciplinary Studies: Where Science and Humanities Meet 124
分野：学際分野
概要：本ユニットでは、大学の学びの中で近年ますます重要度を増している「学際性 (interdisciplinary)」と「国際性 (international)」・「グローバル性 (global)」に焦点を当てる。例えば、環境問題研究 (environmental studies) は、環境を大切にする心や美意識を育む芸術・人間分野 (art・humanities) と問題解決の手段を学ぶ科学 (science) が融合する学際分野であり、また近年注目を集めるナラティブ・メディスン (Narrative Medicine) も、文学と医療からなる「文理融合」分野である。専門の垣根を越えて他分野を学ぶ意義について考えよう。

UNIT 01
Explore the World Beyond the Syllabus*

（＊P.14 の註参照）

新しい扉を開けた向こうに、今まで見たことのない世界が広がる。それが大学生活の第一歩。

Warm-Up

Exchange opinions in pairs or small groups in English. You can use the expressions, words, and phrases below.

1. Do you read the syllabus when you choose courses to take? What kind of information does the syllabus give you?
   Ans.
   ....
   ....

2. What is your major? What would you like to learn at university?
   Ans.
   ....
   ....
   ....

Useful Expressions
My major is…
I would like to learn about…because…
I am interested in…because…
I haven't decided yet, but…

Useful Words and Phrases		
anthropology	education	medicine
art	engineering	philosophy
biology	law	psychology
business administration	linguistics	physics
chemistry	literature	politics
economics	mathematics	sociology

Pre-Reading Vocabulary Check

Match the word to its meaning.

1. admonish	2. anticipate	3. curiosity	4. discipline
5. diploma	6. encounter	7. hesitation	8. resolve
9. wander	10. wonder		

a. to meet or come across someone or something
b. the controlled behavior through training
c. something you receive when you graduate
d. to advise, caution, and encourage someone to do better
e. to let your thoughts go free without conclusion
f. a sense of wanting to know more about something
g. a firm decision on a course of action
h. to walk around with no particular aim in mind
i. the act of pausing before saying or doing something
j. to feel excitement about something happening soon

1		2		3		4		5	
6		7		8		9		10	

Reading

What would you like to learn while at university? Politics? Law? Medicine? Art? Some students major in education to be teachers, and others major in business administration to become business leaders. If you like reading books, you may be interested in taking a literature course. If you love science, you will take science courses without hesitation.

On your very first day on campus, you are told to access the university's website and look at the online course catalog where you will find a long and complicated list of courses and their syllabi.* In other words, it is a collection of all the classes offered at your university. The content of each is explained in the syllabus.* At first glance the course catalog* may look like a shopping catalog, but it's much more than that.

Tatsuru Uchida, Professor Emeritus of Kobe College, reminds us not to think of the course catalog as a place to shop around for classes. There is a big difference between the course catalog and the shopping catalog. The shopping catalog or website gives you access to products you wish to buy. The course catalog, on the other hand, lets you begin thinking about what you want to learn. Moreover, Professor Uchida advises us that much of what you can learn at university cannot be found in the syllabus. In fact, exploring on your own outside of the syllabus is what a university education is all about.* So how do you go about* that?

You begin by exploring the campus and noticing what sparks your interest. At first, you feel totally lost. Not to worry. This is when the learning process kicks in.* All you need to do is to follow your curiosity. Wandering around with your curiosity at the highest level, you will surely encounter something that attracts your attention, for no particular reason.* It might be people dancing on

『街場の教育論』著者の内田樹先生（凱風館館長、神戸女学院大学文学部名誉教授、武道家）

syllabi
syllabus の複数形

syllabus
講義概要、授業計画表。

course catalog
講義要項。大学や学部全体の各講義の syllabus を集めたもの。

what ~ is all about
〜の本質、〜の肝腎なところ

go about
〜にとりかかる。

kick in
（口語表現で）始動する。

for no particular reason
特にこれという理由もなく、なんとなく。

an empty stage, or a group of your seniors having a discussion in the cafeteria. As you wander past a laboratory, you notice students and a professor conducting an experiment. You wonder what these people are doing and why it attracts your attention. At such a moment, you take a first step toward "learning." Your curiosity brings you in contact with the unknown.* Now, take the next step. Ask those dancing students if they don't mind you joining in. Call on your courage and ask the team in the lab what kind of experiment they're up to. Be open to the moment, meet people, and engage with new ideas. This is the way to learning.

    An important next step is to look for a mentor.* You need the guidance of a person with knowledge and experience in order to learn something new. A teacher, friend, or even favorite author or artist can become your mentor. Mentors encourage, admonish, and guide you through their lectures, talks, books, or music. Professor Uchida points out that a mentor helps you make a "breakthrough.*"

    Two good examples are Obi Wan Kenobi and Yoda in *Star Wars*. In *Episode IV: A New Hope*, Luke Skywalker meets Obi Wan, his first mentor, and learns how to handle a light-saber* and become one with "the Force." At first, Luke doubts the effectiveness of these tools. He hasn't experienced their full power yet. Under the guidance of his mentor, though, he begins training as a Jedi and eventually is able to achieve a breakthrough. In *Episode V: The Empire Strikes Back*, Luke meets another mentor, Yoda. Yoda helps Luke realize how much he has yet to learn.* And so with new resolve and self-discipline Luke becomes a mighty Jedi fighter. Finally, in *Episode VI: Return of the Jedi*, after long and disciplined training with Yoda, Luke makes another breakthrough in which he matures not only as a fighter but also as a person. To sum up, you will achieve higher aims with a mentor's guidance.

---

the unknown
知られていない人、未知の人。「the＋形容詞」で「〜な人」の意味になる。
(例) the young = young people 若者たち。

mentor
未熟な者を教え導く熟達者、先達、師匠。

breakthrough
ブレイクスルー。限界を打ち破り新たな境地に至ること。

light-saber
ライトセイバー、光線剣。映画『スター・ウォーズ』シリーズで、ジェダイの騎士たちが操る武器。

how much he has yet to learn
have yet to do で「まだ〜していない」の意味。直訳すると「どれほど彼がまだ学んでいないのか」、つまり「これから彼が学ばなければならないことがまだどれほどあるか」

So, yes, by all means, enjoy selecting classes and planning your schedule. At the same time, keep in mind that learning at university is not about taking classes for four years in order to get a diploma or some kind of certificate that assures you a steady income or social status. Real learning at university begins when you follow your curiosity. Take time to explore the campus. Notice what sparks your interest. Start up a conversation; you never know when and where you will meet your next mentor. Anticipate the breakthrough moment that comes when you combine self-discipline with the guidance of your mentor. Sure, the syllabus lets you know course content, but it cannot be a road map to your unique learning journey. Lift your eyes from the syllabus, go and explore the world around you! (789 words)

付記：本文は、内田樹著『街場の教育論』第3講「キャンパスとメンター」(ミシマ社、2008) の概要を英訳し、解説・解釈を加えたものである。

注記：本文中に言及されている映画『スター・ウォーズ』のエピソードⅣ, Ⅴ, Ⅵは、『スター・ウォーズ』全9作の中で、監督ジョージ・ルーカスが最初に製作した3部作 (original trilogy) で、1977年から83年にかけて公開され世界的大ヒットとなった。主人公ルーク・スカイウォーカーがジェダイの戦士として成長し、帝国軍の支配から宇宙を守る姿が描かれるのだが、その成長は2人の偉大な師 (オビ・ワン・ケノビとその師ヨーダ) の存在なしにはあり得なかった。『スター・ウォーズ』は冒険活劇としての側面が強調されがちだが、若者の成長物語としても優れた作品となっている。

True or False

Decide if each statement below is T (true) or F (false).

1. You should think of the syllabus as a road map that contains everything you will learn at university. T / F
2. An important first step in learning at university is to walk around the campus and notice what attracts your attention. T / F
3. If you see something interesting happening on campus, you should observe carefully from a distance. T / F
4. A mentor is a person whose main responsibility is to correct your mistakes. T / F
5. A breakthrough experience comes to those who, like Luke Skywalker, are lucky. T / F

Comprehension Questions

Answer the questions below.

1. How are the course catalog and shopping catalog different?

2. According to the passage, what do you need to do when you feel lost on the university campus?

3. How does Luke mature as a person as well as a fighter?

Summary

 1-09

Fill in the gaps to complete the summary, then listen to the audio.

Although you're told to access the university's website which has a list of courses and their (1. s_____) on the first day, you mustn't think that it contains everything there is to learn at university. Education at university begins with your (2. c_____). So, the first thing you should do is (3. e_____) the campus and see what (4. s_____) your interest. If you take the time to look around, you'll surely find people doing interesting things. Call on your (5. c_____) and ask what's going on. Secondly, look for a (6. m_____). With a mentor's (7. g_____) you become aware of your lack of (8. k_____) and (9. e_____). Recall Luke Skywalker, who realized that he had a lot more to learn. Only then could he make a (10. b_____).

Discussion and Writing

Do you agree with the idea that university education is about exploring something to learn outside the syllabus? Yes or no? Why? Please share your ideas with your classmates and write a paragraph on this theme.

(a) Your ideas

Agree / Disagree

Reason(s) : _____

_____

_____

(b) Write a paragraph

[Topic   ]

Topic Sentence
Supporting Sentences
Concluding Sentence

Memo

UNIT 02
The University and Civic Engagement: A Brief History

討論する市民。古代ギリシャ／ローマでは公共の広場（アゴラ）で討論、裁判、宗教儀式、商業活動が行われた。

Warm-Up

Exchange opinions in pairs or small groups in English. You can use the expressions, words, and phrases below.

1. Which faculty do you belong to? What got you interested in that area of study?
   Ans.
   ....
   ....

2. What are possible uses for the knowledge and skills you are learning?
   Ans.
   ....
   ....

The University and Civic Engagement: A Brief History — Unit 02

Useful Expressions

I belong to…
I am learning…
My interests include…
I think…will be very useful for my future career because…

Useful Words and Phrases

agriculture	geoscience	nursing
applied sciences	history	nutrition
astronomy	humanities	philosophy
commerce	liberal arts	political science
dentistry	natural sciences	social sciences

Pre-Reading Vocabulary Check

Match the word to its meaning.

1. civic
2. rational
3. voluntary
4. liberate
5. compulsory
6. elective
7. inquiry
8. dialect
9. linguistics
10. symptom

a. to set free
b. a sign of disease
c. mandatory
d. can be chosen, optional
e. research, looking into
f. the study of language
g. of or related to the city or society
h. having to do with the will
i. logical, reasoned, sensible
j. language unique to an area

1		2		3		4		5	
6		7		8		9		10	

Reading

A university's course of studies evolves with the times and needs of the community it serves. In many ways, the purpose of a university education remains much as it was in the days of ancient Greece and Rome: to
5 prepare free citizens for civic duty. Active participation in civic life at that time included public debate on various issues. Success in this required training in three disciplines*: logic, grammar, and rhetoric. Let's take a look at each in turn.

10   Logic guides you in rational ways of thinking. You learn to spot false assumptions and make a reasoned argument. In the discipline of grammar, you learn to speak in well-formed sentences. Sentence types include the statement, question, wish, prayer, command, and
15 exclamation. With these you are able to express rational, voluntary, and emotional states of mind. In the third discipline, rhetoric, you learn the beauty and power of the spoken and written language. Rhetoric includes poetry which appeals to our uniquely human capacity* to
20 imagine and be moved by language. Taken together, the language "arts*" prepared the free citizen's heart and mind for engaging in civic activity.

    These three disciplines, later known as the "trivium*" (three paths crossing), was the starting point of
25 higher education. Developing the heart and mind through the language arts made it possible to know the immaterial world* of truth, goodness, and beauty. The next step was to study the "quadrivium*" (four paths crossing). These were lessons about the material or physical world*, the
30 "sciences" of the day. They were arithmetic, geometry, music (or harmony), and astronomy. The trivium and quadrivium collectively made up the seven disciplines* of the "liberal arts," or the "arts that are liberating."

    Fast forward to the present. The diagram on page
35 24 shows the academic disciplines of a typical university

---

discipline
研究分野における知識

capacity
能力

language arts
言語技能

trivium
〈ラテン語〉〔中世の大学の〕三学科　自由七科のなかの文法（grammar）、修辞学（rhetoric）、論理学（logic）の3科目を指す。

immaterial world
非物質世界、精神世界

quadrivium
〈ラテン語〉〔中世の大学の〕四学科。自由七科のなかの幾何（geometry）、天文（astronomy）、音楽（music）、算術（arithmetic）の4科目を指す。

physical world
物質世界、現実世界

seven disciplines
自由七科、英語では liberal arts

of the present day. As you can see, the number has greatly increased from the original seven of ancient times, mainly in the sciences.

Can you find your major? Keep in mind that this is only a small sample. Your university's catalog will list more. If your major is not listed in the diagram, see if you can determine which of the four categories it would be located in.

The faculty you belong to has its own course of studies. Some classes are compulsory, while others are elective. Be aware also that your department occupies its own domain of knowledge. That is to say, it has its own content, technical terms, and methods of inquiry. There will be overlaps with other faculties, especially among the sciences. The point is: Learn and become practiced in the language and methods of your department. This will lead to success in your academic life and also make you a valuable team member in any discussion, experiment, or fieldwork.

Having mastered your subject, you may feel a desire to branch out into other areas, in which case, you could consider joining an interdisciplinary* research team in the future. This is a group whose members have expertise in different disciplines. By combining their knowledge and skills, the team creates solutions to complex problems. For example, consider the events following Great East Japan Earthquake*, which occurred on March 11, 2011. Emergency response teams* arriving from all over Japan faced a number of unique challenges. One such challenge was providing medical care to elderly patients who could only speak the local dialect. A team was put together with members from the fields of nursing, education, and linguistics. They created a "dialect support tool," a phrasebook of words and expressions for body parts and symptoms in the Tohoku dialect to support communication between the local elderly patients and medical staff not from the area who were unfamiliar with

interdisciplinary
学際的、一分野だけでなく複数の学問分野にまたがっていること

Great East Japan Earthquake
東日本大震災

emergency response team
緊急対応チーム

the dialect.

Interdisciplinary teams are the "new normal," — the smart way to come up with solutions to the complex problems we face today. If you follow the news you can find many examples. Look into a project that interests you and see how what you're learning now at university might change the world. (671 words)

東北方言に国有のオノマトペ（擬音語・擬態語）を集めた用例集。痛みや気持ちを表現する言葉が多く紹介されている。

The Domains of Disciplines in Academic

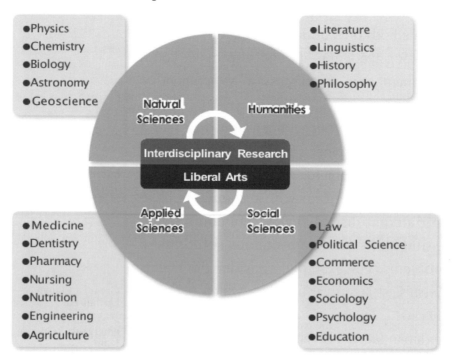

Natural Sciences: Understanding the objects and phenomena of the physical world
Applied Sciences: Applying scientific knowledge to physical problems society faces
Humanities: Understanding the history of knowledge, language, and cultural development
Social Sciences: Applying knowledge of mind and human relations to improve social systems

True or False

Decide if each statement below is T (true) or F (false).

1. The fundamental purpose of a university education has changed a lot over time. **T / F**
2. Education in ancient Greece and Rome aimed to set people free. **T / F**
3. Your department's knowledge domain refers to all the facts you learn. **T / F**
4. An interdisciplinary team is better at solving complex problems. **T / F**
5. You can find out how your studies are relevant by following the news. **T / F**

Comprehension Questions

Answer the questions below.

1. Why was training in the use of language so important in ancient Greece?

2. In any field of study, there are things that students must learn and be able to practice. What are they?

3. What does "new normal" refer to in the passage?

Summary

Fill in the gaps to complete the summary, then listen to the audio.

In the ancient world, university education aimed to prepare citizens for active participation in (1. c_____) life. The core (2. d_____) included the language arts and the sciences. The three language arts developed the (3. m_____), facilitating understanding of truth, goodness, and beauty. The four sciences—arithmetic, geometry, music (or harmony), and astronomy—enabled students to comprehend the (4. p_____) world. Together, these seven disciplines formed the (5. l_____) arts, educating a liberated or free person. Today, the number of academic disciplines has greatly increased, mainly in the (6. s_____). Understanding your department's knowledge domain, including course content, specialist language, and methods of (7. i_____), is crucial. You may be interested in joining an (8. i_____) research team, where members with diverse expertise collaborate to tackle (9. c_____) problems creatively. You can learn how your studies are (10. r_____) by following the news and looking into projects that interest you.

Memo

Discussion and Writing

If you wanted to solve a problem in society, what kind of interdisciplinary project would you launch? Please share your ideas with your classmates and write a paragraph on this theme.

(a) Your ideas

_____

_____

_____

(b) Write a paragraph

[Topic   ]

Topic Sentence
Supporting Sentences
Concluding Sentence

UNIT 03

Life Design for Centenarians*

*Centenarian
100歳（以上）

超高齢化社会到来。人生100年時代におけるライフデザインを考えてみよう。

Warm-Up

Exchange opinions in pairs or small groups in English. You can use the expressions, words, and phrases below.

1. What do you think is the reason for a decline in the mortality rate of the elderly?
   Ans.
   ....
   ....
   ....

2. What would you like to do after retirement?
   Ans.
   ....
   ....
   ....

Life Design for Centenarians* | Unit 03

Useful Expressions
My dream is to…
I would like to … because …
I think I'll … because…
I don't know exactly what I want to do, but …

Useful Words and Phrases	
travel around …	move abroad
live in the country	go on a cruise
do volunteer work	start to learn …
run a café	do gardening

Pre-Reading Vocabulary Check

Match the word to its meaning.

1. phenomenon	2. fertility	3. drastic	4. exceed
5. fortunate	6. defy	7. cognitive	8. statistics
9. prosperous	10. consequence		

   a. the ability to produce babies
   b. be in a good situation or have something good
   c. something that happens in society or nature
   d. a set of numbers which show facts
   e. related to understanding and learning something
   f. extreme or serious
   g. rich and successful
   h. to be more than a particular number or amount
   i. to refuse to obey a rule
   j. a result or effect

1		2		3		4		5	
6		7		8		9		10	

29

Reading

Japan's Place in an Aging World

An aging population refers to the phenomenon in which people 65 years and older make up an increasing percentage of the country's total population. When the proportion of the elderly reaches 7 percent, the country is considered an aging country. The aging of a population results from a decline in the mortality rate of the elderly, along with a decline in the fertility rate. Since the end of the last century, the number of countries with aging populations has increased remarkably and is now a globally recognized phenomenon. In France, the UK, Sweden, and Germany, the aging population percentage grew to over 10 percent as early as 1956. It was in 1970 that Japan became a member of this group, with its elderly reaching 7.1 percent of the total population. In 2005, when this number reached over 20 percent, Japan became the country with the largest proportion of elderly in the world. As of* 2020, the percentage was 29.1 percent. It is expected to reach 35.3 percent in 2040, and 38.4 percent in 2065.

Japan is aging rapidly. A population's aging speed is calculated based on "the doubling of the aging rate,*" that is, the number of years it takes for a country's aging population to double from the base of 7 percent to 14 percent. While it took France 126 years for its aging population to double, it took Japan only 24 years. This is one of the most rapid increases of all countries worldwide in history. As a consequence of this rapid aging, Japan has been forced to make drastic changes in its social security and social welfare systems (e.g. pensions* and health care), and it has done so in an extremely short period of time.

21st Century Japan Achieves the Dream of a Long Life

In the Meiji and the Taisho eras, the average life expectancy of Japanese was early 40s. In 1947, the

81歳でゲームアプリを開発し、世界最高齢のプログラマーとして活躍する若宮正子氏。

As of
〜時点で

the doubling of the aging rate
倍加年数

pensions
年金

average life expectancy reached 50.06 years for men, and 53.96 years for women. It was the first time that the average life expectancy for both men and women exceeded 50 years. Living past this age was an accomplishment.* Only 40 percent of men and 50 percent of women in Japan in 1947 lived past the age of 65. These years were considered to be a person's "remaining years,*" and only the most fortunate in society were able to achieve such longevity. Since then, the average life expectancy has continued to increase greatly. As of 2021, it was 81.47 years for men and 87.57 years for women. The average life expectancy is expected to increase even more, reaching 84.95 for men, and 91.35 for women by 2065. These numbers show that the Japanese in the 21st century have achieved what has long been a dream of mankind, a longer life. Having achieved such a long-life span, it is now important to consider how these elder members of society will spend their later years.*

accomplishment
偉業

remaining years
余生

later years
晩年

Design for Life in the 90s

These days, the elderly in Japan not only live longer, but have also become "younger" both physically and mentally, seeming to defy their chronological age.* For example, over the past 10 years the average walking speed of an elderly person has increased. A 75-year-old now walks at the same speed as a 64-year-old 10 years ago. This pattern is also true for cognitive ability. Recent scores on an intelligence test of people in their 60s were close to the results of 40- and 50-year-olds 10 years ago. Scores of people in their 70s come close to those of people in their 60s 10 years ago. Recently, the number of active elderly people with "*ikigai*," a reason for being, has been increasing. The time has come to start a discussion on whether to redefine the term "elderly," which currently refers to a person of 65 years or older.

These days, the later years in one's life can no

chronological age
暦年齢

longer be considered the "remaining years," reserved only for those who are the most fortunate. As of 2020, statistics show that approximately 28.1 percent of men and 52.6 percent of women live to be 90 years old. Some authoritative demographers* in the U.S. and Germany even predict that 50 percent of the Japanese born in 2007 will live to be over 107. Given these numbers, we should think more seriously about how we could make our life in our 90s and 100s active, meaningful, and even prosperous. (746 words)

demographers
人口学者

True or False

Decide if each statement below is T (true) or F (false).

1. Japan became a member of the group of aging countries in the mid-1950s. **T / F**
2. It was in 1947 when the average life expectancy for both men and women exceeded 50 years for the first time. **T / F**
3. As of 2021, the average life expectancy for women is longer than that for men. **T / F**
4. Recent scores on an intelligence test of people in their 60s were much worse than the results of 40- and 50-year-olds 10 years ago. **T / F**
5. We may have to redefine the term "elderly," because there are more active people these days, including those even over the age of 65. **T / F**

Life Design for Centenarians* Unit 03

Comprehension Questions

Answer the questions below.

1. What are two reasons for the aging of a population?

2. How is a population's aging speed calculated?

3. What do some demographers predict about the future life span of Japanese people?

Summary

 1-24

Fill in the gaps to complete the summary, then listen to the audio.

Since the end of the last century, the number of countries with aging populations has increased (**1. r**_____). Japan has experienced one of the most (**2. r**_____) increases of its aging population of all countries. As a result, Japan has had to change its social security systems and social (**3. w**_____) systems. Average life (**4. e**_____) has continued to increase greatly. It is expected to reach 84.95 for men and 91.35 for women (**5. b**___) 2065. It is important to consider how these elderly people will spend their (**6. l**_____) years. These days, the elderly in Japan have become "younger" both (**7. p**_____) and (**8. m**_____). Moreover, the number of (**9. a**_____) elderly people has been increasing. We should prepare ourselves for our (**10. p**_____) 90s and 100s.

33

Discussion and Writing

When you are 100 years old, what do you think the world will be like? What will be possible then? Will you be living a happy life? Please share your ideas with your classmates and write a paragraph on this theme.

(a) Your ideas

_____

_____

_____

(b) Write a paragraph

[Topic   ]

Topic Sentence

Supporting Sentences

Concluding Sentence

Memo

UNIT 04
Can Humans Really Fall in Love with Robots?

見つめ合う人間とAIロボット―両者の間に果たして「共感」や「愛情」は芽生えるのだろうか？

Warm-Up

Exchange opinions in pairs or small groups in English. You can use the expressions, words, and phrases below.

1. What is AI?
   Ans. ....
   ....
   ....

2. What do you think is one use of AI? How would you like to apply AI to your life?
   Ans. ....
   ....
   ....

Can Humans Really Fall in Love with Robots? **Unit 04**

Useful Expressions

The thing that interests me about AI is…
I would like to learn about AI because…
I will give you some good / bad examples of AI…
I think in the future AI will…

Useful Words and Phrases

autonomy	future	society
algorithm	technology	robot
intelligence	engineering	communication
usefulness	programming	efficiency
relationship	randomness	aging
marriage	language	artificial intelligence
		machine translation

Pre-Reading Vocabulary Check

Match the word to its meaning.

1. autonomous	2. commonplace	3. programming	4. substitute
5. AI	6. develop	7. parameter	8. intimate
9. system	10. self-determination		

a. to progress or to grow into a more advanced form
b. a thing or person that is used instead of another thing or person
c. developing computer systems that try to reproduce human intelligence
d. having the freedom from external control or influence
e. involving very close connection
f. the instructions that tell a computer what to do
g. not considered unusual
h. a set of things working together as parts of a mechanism
i. a set of facts or a fixed limit
j. the ability to make decisions by oneself

1		2		3		4		5	
6		7		8		9		10	

Reading

AI (Artificial Intelligence) has become an essential component of our daily lives, being widely used in such fields as medical and home devices, video games, autonomous cars, and robots. AI systems have now
5 acquired the ability to teach themselves. For example, when used in so-called* deep-learning,* AI applications have developed to the point where machines can teach themselves and even make decisions on their own.

AI will change our lives, but questions must be
10 asked. One question is who will control the machines? A second question is how will we control this technology? Every advance in technology changes humanity's relationship with nature. In this case we are discussing human nature, and AI may change the very way that*
15 human beings relate to each other emotionally. Is this a good thing?

What will our brave new world* look like? Some experts say that AI will allow some people to replace their need for intimate human relationships by emotional and
20 physical intimacy with robots in virtual reality. Perhaps this is understandable because relationships with human beings are difficult, filled with each individual's shortcomings, often messy, and even hazardous. Can AI replace this most basic of human needs? Will we create
25 our own perfect virtual companions in the future? Will a machine become our spiritual soul mate? Are these realistic questions? Next, we will consider the possibility of marriage between humans and robots.

In the future, humans may find it perfectly natural
30 to fall in love with robots. The notion of robophilia* may help explain this. One meaning of this notion is that robots could become sexually attractive to humans. Certainly, if humanoid robots begin to increasingly resemble humans, feelings of love between humans and
35 robots may become commonplace someday in the future.

---

so-called
いわゆる
deep-learning
深層学習：人間の行動（画像や音声認識、翻訳等）をコンピューターに学習させる機械学習の一つ

the very way that~
まさに～のやり方そのもの

brave new world
未来社会。ただし、イギリスの小説家、オールダス・ハクスリー (Aldous Huxley) が1932年に発表したディストピア小説、*Brave New World*『素晴らしい新世界』を連想させる。

robophilia
ロボットを対象とした恋愛感情（性的なものを含む）

Here we need to think about the nature of love. There are so many forms of love relationships in societies and cultures that it is difficult to assert that one particular form of physical and emotional intimacy is right or wrong. If a human develops a physical or emotional bond with a robot that is programmed to resemble a human, can we presume that this relationship is wrong? In short, it might not be unreasonable to expect that people may develop emotional bonds with robots.

Why then would some humans choose to have feelings of love for robots rather than for other humans? One main reason is that in this kind of relationship, you can create your own custom-made robots.* Depending on how you choose to program it, you can freely determine how deep and emotional your relationship with a robot is. You can create one that is perfect only for you, both physically and emotionally. Programming can make your dream come true, and you can create your ideal mate based on your own parameters. This robot you have created may always give you positive feedback, thus eliminating the pain that is often characteristic of relationships between humans. However, is this really the ideal relationship you crave? In a relationship between you and a robot, you may transfer yourself onto your robot partner*, but the reverse does not happen. This seems narcissistic. In this regard, it would be helpful to consider the idea of self-determination. AI can be defined as operating according to a deterministic algorithm*, which eliminates randomness*, whereas human nature can be characterized by randomness.

Let's try to expand our discussion: is marriage possible between humans and robots? Of course, questions about the legal aspects of this have to be solved, and it would take a long time for people to be persuaded that this kind of marriage should be allowed. However, one big problem could be how AI changes the notion of what it means to be human. Humans themselves invented

create your own custom-made robots
あなた好みのロボットをオーダーメイドのように創り上げる

transfer yourself onto your robot partner
自分をロボットのパートナーに投影する

deterministic algorithm
決定的アルゴリズム。入力を与えられたとき、常に同じ結果を返すこと

randomness
予測不可能な状態：無作為性

AI, but in the future, AI may even surpass them to become their master. This may cause ethical problems.

In this unit, you are asked to have your own answer or opinion regarding the following questions. Will it be possible for humans to develop long term relationships with robots? If so, how will this be understood legally? And how should we look at this kind of relationship? Can a robot be a substitute for a mother or father and nurture children to maturity?*   (707 words)

nurture children to maturity
子供を立派な大人に育て上げる

世界的なロボット研究者である石黒浩氏は、ロボットを作ることは「人間とは何か」を考えることだと述べる。

True or False

Decide if each statement below is T (true) or F (false).

1. Marriage between humans and robots will soon be allowed by the Japanese government. T / F
2. AI can have ethical problems, because as to intelligence, AI may be superior to humans in the future. T / F
3. Humans may feel love for robots, but the opposite may not be true. T / F
4. Love relationships between humans and robots are not possible because the physical appearances of the two are still too different from one another. T / F
5. AI can give us a good opportunity to rethink such topics as friendship or marriage. T / F

Comprehension Questions

Answer the questions below.

1. What items are mentioned as examples of AI devices in this passage?

2. According to the author, what is one of the main reasons why some humans may feel love for robots?

3. The author maintains that the love relationship between you and robots tends to be narcissistic. What explanations does the author give in the passage?

Summary

1-32

Fill in the gaps to complete the summary, then listen to the audio.

AI has become (**1.** e_____) for our daily (**2.** l_____) in recent years. Some experts (**3.** m_____) AI can be created as a (**4.** s_____) for humans. This means humans may be able to have close (**5.** r_____) and (**6.** f_____) in love with robots in the (**7.** f_____). However, there are many (**8.** c_____) problems with this kind of relationship. Only programmed algorithms can be used to provide (**9.** s_____) responses to feelings of love. Even if robots are created to look and act like humans, there are still many problems left to consider. (**10.** E_____) is only one of the key issues among such problems.

Discussion and Writing

Do you approve of the marriage between humans and robots? Please share your ideas with your classmates and write a paragraph on this theme.

(a) Your ideas

_____

_____

_____

(b) Write a paragraph

[Topic   ]

Topic Sentence
Supporting Sentences
Concluding Sentence

Memo

UNIT 05
Business in Asia: Global Talents in Japan

日本ポタジエブランドのプロジェクトを、アジア太平洋地域において「橋渡し＝ブリッジング」する河合氏（右）とパートナーのJerry氏（左）。

Warm-Up

Exchange opinions in pairs or small groups in English. You can use the expressions, words, and phrases below.

1. Please describe someone who works overseas. He or she can be your friend, a family member, or celebrities such as athletes or actors, etc.
   Ans. ....
   ....

2. Would you like to work overseas?
   Ans. ....
   ....

44

Useful Expressions

I would like to … because …
My goal is …
A friend of mine … and …
I don't really want to work overseas, but …
I love to stay inside my country, because …

Useful Words and Phrases

have broad knowledge	work as a volunteer
experience various cultures	save children
learn different languages	I'm interested in international business
meet diverse people	prefer local cultures

Pre-Reading Vocabulary Check

Match the word to its meaning.

1. fulfill
2. dominate
3. hereditary
4. seniority
5. indispensable
6. emphasize
7. artisans
8. subtitles
9. goods
10. venture

a. to control someone
b. to say something in a strong way
c. words on a screen translating what is being said
d. products
e. being older or higher in rank than someone else
f. craftsmen
g. to achieve, carry out
h. passed from a parent to a child
i. necessary, extremely important
j. a business enterprise, typically one that involves risk

| 1 | | 2 | | 3 | | 4 | | 5 | |
| 6 | | 7 | | 8 | | 9 | | 10 | |

Reading

Is Cool Japan a helpful attitude to developing business in Asia? Interview with a global talent.

Mr. Tomohiro Kawai, President of Potager Asia-Pacific,* is pushing overseas expansion of his company, a manufacturer of vegetable sweets based in Nakameguro, Tokyo. He is fulfilling the role of "bridging" Japan and Asia by setting up joint ventures* with local companies in Asia.

Interviewer: What is important in your work?

Mr. Kawai: It is important to balance localization and globalization. There are several reasons why we develop our business in a local way rather than a Japanese style. In order to make a business successful in Asia, you may think that you need to develop products which meet local needs. As highly skilled artisans, many Japanese companies try to sell goods that they believe are wonderful from a Japanese point of view, but they are not always successful. My company's policy is to act flexibly. By that I mean we adapt our products to local circumstances. If you sell your products just as they are, you cannot win the hearts of the local customers. On the other hand, you cannot sell something that is already common in that foreign country, because it is not exciting to the local people any more. In the field of business, global human resources can be defined as people who have knowledge of both localization and globalization and can balance those opposites.*

Interviewer: So, is your policy consistent throughout Asia?

Mr. Kawai: The situation is different in each country. For example, the Philippines is tolerant of foreign cultures, probably because of the historical fact that it was dominated by Spain and the United States. Meanwhile, Thailand has never become a colony, and respect for the

Potager Asia-Pacific
ポタジエ・アジア・パシフィック、東京中目黒を拠点に野菜スイーツを製造する会社

joint ventures
合弁会社

opposites
正反対のもの

royal family is strong, so they will not let go of their culture.* However, as in other Asian countries such as Singapore, Malaysia, Indonesia, and Vietnam, overseas Chinese* have a great deal of influence in these countries.

Interviewer: So do you develop your business in a Chinese way?

Mr. Kawai: Partly, yes. To achieve business success in these countries, you need to know their cultural background. People there are family-oriented,* and their companies basically have a hereditary structure. If the head of the family does not say okay, nothing goes forward. Three factors are important for business in Asia: big familyism*, seniority, and being a good friend. For example, when negotiating with an Asian company, I never contact the department in charge directly. Instead I meet elderly people at the company. When I meet older Chinese there, I speak Chinese. Of course, I speak English to negotiate with the people in charge, who are overseas Chinese from the younger generation. For me, Japanese, English, and Chinese are indispensable tools for developing business in Asia.

Interviewer: Is language skill significant when collecting information for your business?

Mr. Kawai: I collect information in Japanese, English, and Chinese. I often watch the BBC and Channel News Asia in Singapore in English. I also watch the Taiwanese news with Chinese subtitles and read a newspaper called the *South China Morning Post* from Hong Kong. If I don't know which political party my business partner supports, my business may not work out. I always put out feelers* for information beyond business. You need to understand local circumstances and needs before selling your products, no matter how good their quality may be. Language is an essential tool when collecting necessary information in this respect.*

---

not let go of their culture
自国の文化を手放さない

overseas Chinese
華僑

family-oriented
家族中心主義の

big familyism
大家族主義

put out feelers
アンテナを張る

respect
点

Interviewer: Could you tell us about your marketing strategy in Asia?

Mr. Kawai: You must change your marketing strategy from country to country. Potager is a company that offers sweets from France. When marketing in Japan, we emphasize the healthy aspects of vegetable sweets. On the other hand, in the Philippines and Thailand, where the health market is not as established as in Japan, we put the stylish image of French sweets out in front. Taiwan is friendly toward Japan, and we emphasize that our products are Japanese. In marketing in the Philippines, you need to consider the fact that American culture is influential there. In this way, your strategy should be changed according to the cultural background of each country.

If you work overseas, you may need to find international personnel* who are familiar with the local culture. I would say flexibility is the key to success in global business. Japanese manufacturers have a strong sense of craftsmanship*, and are proud of their skills and qualities. However, since other Asian countries such as China and South Korea can now produce items with the same quality, you cannot attract consumers by quality alone. What Japanese companies need is a flexible way of thinking. Starting with marketing of sweets, we are now expanding our business to advertisements, music, and artistic productions. If you have a flexible mind, I believe you can fulfill a bridging role between point A and point B regardless of your type of job. (821 words)

personnel
人、人員

a sense of craftsmanship
職人気質

シンガポールの中央ビジネス地区にあるチャイナタウン。シンガポールでは総人口の約4分の3が華僑（中華系の住民）である。

Business in Asia: Global Talents in Japan | Unit 05

True or False

Decide if each statement below is T (true) or F (false).

1. In Thailand people strongly respect the royal family. T / F
2. Mr. Kawai contacts the department in charge directly when he wants to negotiate with a company. T / F
3. Mr. Kawai tries to know about the political situation when he reads local newspapers, in order to be trusted by business partners and to get them to cooperate with his business. T / F
4. Potager emphasizes Japanese style when they sell their products in Taiwan. T / F
5. People who are familiar with the cultural background of a country may be required in international businesses. T / F

Comprehension Questions

Answer the questions below.

1. In the field of business, how can global human resources be defined?

2. Who is influential in the business world of Asian countries such as Singapore and Malaysia?

3. What has a great influence on the marketing in the Philippines?

Summary

1-40

Fill in the gaps to complete the summary, then listen to the audio.

Mr. Kawai is trying to build a (**1.** b_____) between a Japanese business and local companies in Asia. If he wants to make his business (**2.** s_____) in Asia, he needs to know the cultural background. For example, familyism, (**3.** s_____), and being a good friend are very important (**4.** f_____) for businesses in Asia. The market background also varies (**5.** a_____) to the country. He has to change his market (**6.** s_____) in each country. In addition, (**7.** f_____) is required in order to (**8.** g_____) local needs. The important thing is to understand what (**9.** l_____) and (**10.** g_____) are and have the ability to combine or adjust them.

Discussion and Writing

What kind of image do you think other Asian people have of Japan? Please share your ideas with your classmates and write a paragraph on this theme.

(a) Your ideas

_____

_____

_____

(b) Write a paragraph

[Topic   ]

Topic Sentence
Supporting Sentences
Concluding Sentence

〈参考〉
The Straits Times: https://www.straitstimes.com/global　　シンガポールの新聞
Focus Taiwan: http://focustaiwan.tw　　中国や台湾関連のニュースが豊富
CNA: https://www.channelnewsasia.com/news/international　　日本関連のビデオクリップが豊富

Memo

UNIT 06
What Literary Works Teach Us

バーナード・ショーが1905年から亡くなる1950年まで住んだ家。ロンドンの北ハートフォードシャーにあり、通称ショーズコーナーと呼ばれて一般公開されている。

Warm-Up

Exchange opinions in pairs or small groups in English. You can use the expressions, words, and phrases below.

1. Do you enjoy reading books written in English? If yes, what kind of books do you enjoy reading? If no, why not?
   Ans.

2. What is your impression of literature in general? Do you enjoy reading literary works?
   Ans.

What Literary Works Teach Us — Unit 06

Useful Expressions

I think literature is …
My favorite author is …
I enjoy reading… in my free time.
I do not read literary works because…
I like reading literary works because…

Useful Words and Phrases

interesting	reflect on society	enjoyable	help me grow
fun	evoke emotions	inspiring	experience
creative	poem	boring	novel

Pre-Reading Vocabulary Check

Match the word to its meaning.

1. adaptation   2. transform   3. sequel   4. enfeeble
5. interpret   6. expository   7. evaluate 8. authentic
9. infer   10. grapple

a. not false; real
b. to give the meaning of
c. a movie or play that was first written in a different form, for example, as a book
d. to form an opinion that something is probably true
e. explaining and describing something
f. to try hard to deal with a difficult problem
g. to carefully consider something to make a judgment
h. to completely change the appearance, form, or character
i. to make someone weak
j. a book, movie, play, etc. that continues the story of an earlier one, usually written or created by the same person

| 1 | | 2 | | 3 | | 4 | | 5 | |
| 6 | | 7 | | 8 | | 9 | | 10 | |

Reading

George Bernard Shaw's *Pygmalion* is a famous play that owes much of its fame to its film adaptation as *My Fair Lady*. In the play, Eliza Doolittle was a poor flower girl who spoke in her local dialect. The phonetician,* Professor Higgins, transformed her into a fine "lady" who spoke upper-middle class English. The work is known for the example of accent modification* and also as a typical Cinderella-type story.

However, the fact that Shaw rewrote the ending of his original play and added a sequel in the 1916 printed text is not widely known. Shaw, who strove* to bring a new sense of realism to British drama, could not support the "happy ending" scenario expected of romances at that time. He was shocked to see the actor playing Higgins toss a bouquet of flowers to Eliza on the stage, suggesting a future marriage. In response, Shaw insisted that Eliza marry Freddy* instead of Higgins and wrote that story in the sequel. We can read his strong claim in the first sentence in "Sequel," that is, "The rest of the story need not be shown in action,* and indeed, would hardly need telling if our imaginations were not so enfeebled by their lazy dependence on the ready-makes* and reach-me-downs* of the ragshop* in which Romance keeps its stock of 'happy endings' to misfit all stories."

This demonstrates one of the important characteristics of literary texts: everyone, including readers, actors (in this case), and the author, might differently interpret a text. In *Pygmalion*, the actor did not play the part as the author had envisioned* it probably because of a commercial reason, and the author was concerned that audiences and readers might interpret the ending of the play in a way he had not intended. In a case like this, even the author might lose control, and thus literature allows people to personally interpret what they read and to create their own meanings. It is true that

---

phonetician
音声学者

modification
修正

strove
strive の過去形
〜しようと努力する

Freddy
イライザに一目惚れし、彼女に純粋な恋心を抱く没落した上流階級の若者。経済的には無力で頼りない。原作『ピグマリオン』のSequelでイライザと結婚することが描かれる。
in action
劇の形で
ready-makes
出来合いの服
reach-me-downs
着古し
ragshop
古着屋

envision
心に描く

literary works might be more freely read than expository or informative texts, which we usually read in order to collect information. Therefore, by reading literary works, we can learn that people often have different understandings as well as various opinions and interpretations of things, and that it is important to tolerate* alternative beliefs and attitudes. Simultaneously, we become better prepared to face challenging problems. It is illusory* to believe that there always is one correct answer to any question, perhaps particularly in our complex modern society, which is full of controversial* issues.

In the context of learning a foreign language, literary works have been highly evaluated mainly in the United Kingdom since the 1980s, based on research findings in stylistics* and other related subject areas. "Literature" was redefined as a wider range of writings including novels, poetry, plays, and screenplays adapted in films and dramas. It is argued that literature is beneficial in increasing language awareness and promoting personal growth. It could also give learners cultural knowledge about the place where the target language is spoken. In the classroom, literary texts or a film adaptation of a literary work can be useful resources that offer various language tasks and activities such as discussion and creative writing. Some research even suggests effectiveness of using literature in fostering awareness of spoken language or improving speaking skills. These studies regard literature as an authentic material that develops communicative competence, which might not be well acknowledged in Japan.

In addition to all those features, as you learned in the example of *Pygmalion* above, literature gives learners opportunities to express themselves and stimulates the imagination. It also helps them develop critical thinking skills as literature requires learners to infer meaning and interpret situations from the unstated implications* and

tolerate
許容する

illusory
錯覚の

controversial
論争となる

stylistics
文体論：特に文学作品の文体を研究する学問分野

implication
言外の意味、含意

assumptions in the texts. By grappling with the multiple ambiguities* in literary texts, you may be trained to enhance your interpretative and inferential skills and to apply them to your other studies at university as well.

Perhaps it is almost impossible to distinguish sharply literary texts from non-literary ones, but literature is likely to play a significant role both in language learning and in our lives. We should reconsider what literary works teach us and try to expose our minds to many different types of texts including literature. We may be able to learn our target language in a more meaningful way than before, and at the same time, learn valuable lessons from literature as a person. (737 words)

ambiguity
多義性、あいまいさ

ロンドンにあるコベントガーデンの様子。劇場街に近くいつも大勢の人で賑わっている。戯曲ピグマリオンで、音声学者のヒギンズ教授は花売り娘のイライザとここで出会った。

True or False

Decide if each statement below is T (true) or F (false).

1. *My Fair Lady* is a famous film based on the play titled *Pygmalion*.　　T / F
2. Shaw supported the happy ending because the play was a romance.　　T / F
3. Shaw insisted that Eliza marry Higgins at the end of the play.　　T / F
4. Literary works might be more freely read than expository or informative texts.　　T / F
5. Literary texts play an important role in language learning only because they offer various language tasks and activities.　　T / F

Unit 06 — What Literary Works Teach Us

Comprehension Questions

Answer the questions below.

1. What did Bernard Shaw do when he published *Pygmalion* in 1916?

2. What are some benefits of literature in language learning?

3. What kind of language activities do literary texts offer in the language classroom?

Summary

 1-47

Fill in the gaps to complete the summary, then listen to the audio.

When we learn about Bernard Shaw's writing a (**1.** s_____) to his famous play *Pygmalion*, we notice one of the important characteristics that literary texts have: they often allow people to (**2.** i_____) what they read and create personal meanings. Therefore, by reading literary works, we can learn that people often have different understandings, and various opinions and (**3.** i_____) of things, and that it is important to (**4.** t_____) (**5.** a_____) beliefs and (**6.** a_____). (**7.** S_____), we can be better prepared to face challenging problems. In the context of learning a foreign language, literary texts appear to play a (**8.** s_____) role not only because they offer a variety of language tasks and activities but also because they help learners (**9.** e_____) their interpretative and (**10.** i_____) skills.

Discussion and Writing

Please think about the literary work or movie which you like best, including the title, a summary, how it influenced you, and so on. Please share your ideas with your classmates and write a paragraph on this theme.

(a) Your ideas

_____

_____

_____

(b) Write a paragraph

[Topic   ]

Topic Sentence
Supporting Sentences
Concluding Sentence

Memo

UNIT 07

Advice from the Philosopher Nietzsche: Have a Strong Will to Live Well

ニーチェが教える現代に生きるヒントとは？
古代ギリシャ人の悲劇の捉え方から学ぶ。

Warm-Up

Exchange opinions in pairs or small groups in English. You can use the expressions, words, and phrases below.

1. What do you enjoy doing yourself when you have free time?
   Ans.
   ....
   ....
   ....

2. Do you have some favorite words or phrases to give you courage or hope? If so, what are they?
   Ans.
   ....
   ....
   ....

Advice from the Philosopher Nietzsche: Have a Strong Will to Live Well   Unit 07

Useful Expressions
I like …   I am interested in …   My hobby is …   What I like to do is …

Useful Words and Phrases	
taking photos	going to karaoke
reading books	listening to my favorite music
travel	talking with my friends
cooking	going out for shopping

Pre-Reading Vocabulary Check

Match the word to its meaning.

1. blame	2. failure	3. goal	4. courage
5. behavior	6. disappointment	7. destiny	8. struggle
9. cruel	10. theatrical		

a. fate; the things that will happen or have happened
b. causing pain and unhappiness
c. to feel that something or someone has the cause for a fault or wrong
d. to try very hard; have a hard fight
e. sadness because something has failed to happen
f. the way one acts
g. lack of success
h. something that you want to achieve; purpose, aim
i. bravery, strength in the face of pain
j. connected with the theater

1		2		3		4		5	
6		7		8		9		10	

Reading

　　How would you feel if you failed the interview for the company at which you most wanted to work? You might blame yourself, saying that you were not good enough for the job. That could happen to everyone. How would you feel if you were rejected when you declared your love to the person of your dreams? You might think you will never want to fall in love again. Such feelings are natural.

　　The German philosopher Nietzsche* says that life is full of troubles and problems that come one after another. In other words, life is full of failures and mistakes, and it always brings disappointment and sadness. So, you could say, in low spirits, "That's life. Let's forget about it." You could give up on what you want to do with your life and do nothing about it. On the other hand, you could say positively, "That's life. Let's try again." You could take a step forward toward your life's goals.

　　Nietzsche teaches us how to live our own lives just as we like, because he thinks living a life of your own is the best way to make yourself happy. He tells us that we have to get over problems and troubles with courage. He also believes that it is very important for you to make up your mind* to be successful in what you want to do in your life. Of course, he knows that living just as you wish is actually very difficult.

　　Nietzsche gives us some advice on how to have a strong will and live well. In his first philosophical work,* he takes up the ancient Greeks as the perfect example of how life goes on, even though we are hurt or disappointed. In *The Birth of Tragedy*,* he writes that the Greek tragedy written by such poets as Sophocles* and Aeschylus* reveals what life is like.

　　In ancient Greece, watching and performing theatrical plays was not only a recreation for ordinary people but also a sacred ceremony for the gods and

---

Nietzsche
フリードリヒ・ニーチェ (1844–1900) ドイツ出身の哲学者

make up your mind
決心する

philosophical work
哲学書
The Birth of Tragedy
『悲劇の誕生』(1872年) ニーチェによる著作
Sophocles
ソポクレス (496–406 B.C.) ギリシャの悲劇詩人
Aeschylus
アイスキュロス (525–456 B.C.) ギリシャの悲劇詩人

goddesses of Olympus.* The genre of tragedy was important above all others.* In tragedies, stories from mythology* were popular. Using mythology, the plays expressed the meaning of life to the audience.

In Greek mythology, the gods and goddesses of Olympus live in the same way as humans do. Sometimes they get angry at the rude behavior of humans, who have no respect for gods and goddesses, and inflict* severe punishment on them. Before the great power of the gods, humans are faced with the harsh realities of destiny. They are forced to think deeply about what was wrong with their actions and feel sorry for what they have done.

However, if you come to know that we cannot live without making mistakes and that we were born this way, it may help you to find your path in life a little more easily. Nietzsche says that the violence of gods' anger at humans shows the power of the ancient Greeks' personalities. The Greeks of those days already knew that life in its natural state* was cruel and savage, and sometimes it was far beyond their control. On the other hand, the Greeks always tried to control their behavior and to keep themselves in good order.* They also had a strong sense of beauty.

Nietzsche calls the former characteristics the Dionysian, and the latter the Apollonian. "Dionysian" comes from Dionysus, who was originally a Greek god of fertility and was later worshiped as a god of wine. Dionysus was also respected as the symbol of the freedom of feelings and freedom from shyness and self-consciousness. As for "Apollonian," it comes from Apollo, the god of music, poetic inspiration, archery, prophecy,* medicine, and the sun. Thus, the god Apollo is associated with the power of the mind to think in a logical way.

Nietzsche explains that these two opposed qualities struggle with each other and in the end become one within the character of the Greeks. That is, tragedy written by Greek authors is the fruit* of these two opposing forces. The same thing can be said about Greek mythology as well. Ancient Greeks enjoyed watching works of tragedy in the theater and felt refreshed by them. It made them think that life was full of sad events, and they said to each other, "Life goes on."

If you have ever attempted to do something but failed, the result might have made you very unhappy. This is certainly a sad thing. However, what Nietzsche calls real tragedy is when you give in to* the temptation to stop trying. If you never give up your goal in life, Nietzsche will be by your side, saying: first, find the path you really want to take; second, believe in yourself; and finally remember that making mistakes is a part of human condition, and taking a second chance is a part of human life.　　　　　　　　　　　　　　　　(817 words)

give in to ~
〜に負ける

観劇は古代ギリシャ人の娯楽であり、ストレス解消法でもあった。

True or False

Decide if each statement below is T (true) or F (false).

1. Nietzsche is also a German writer of tragedies.　　　　　　　　　　T / F
2. In ancient Greece, stories from mythology were performed at the Olympic Games.　　　　　　　　　　T / F
3. Nietzsche explained that Greeks could be divided into either rational people or emotional people.　　　　　　　　　　T / F
4. Nietzsche says that life is full of sad events, so it is wise to accept it just as it is and do nothing about it.　　　　　　　　　　T / F
5. According to Nietzsche, emotional things are called "Dionysian," while matters of rule and order are called "Apollonian."　　　　　　　　　　T / F

Comprehension Questions

Answer the questions below.

1. What is the god Apollo associated with?

2. How did ancient Greeks refresh themselves?

3. According to Nietzsche, what is real tragedy?

Summary

 1-58

Fill in the gaps to complete the summary, then listen to the audio.

The German (**1. p**_____) Nietzsche explains that making (**2. m**_____) is a part of human condition, so life is full of problems. However, the philosopher advises us to have the (**3. c**_____) to overcome troubles and take a step forward toward the (**4. a**_____) of our life. He takes up the ancient Greeks as a good example of how to live a life of your own, even though we face sad (**5. e**_____) one after another. In ancient Greece, enjoying theatrical plays was a common (**6. r**_____) for ordinary people. According to Nietzsche, (**7. t**_____) was more important than any other genre, because Greek tragedy expressed the (**8. m**_____) of life to the audience. What he calls real tragedy is that, once a negative (**9. e**_____) has made you unhappy, you really give up everything. So, Nietzsche says taking a second (**10. c**_____) will make you happy again.

Discussion and Writing

A lot of people have some favorite words or phrases that give them power or hope. They are called "mottos." What is your motto? How does it encourage you? Please share your ideas with your classmates and write a paragraph on this theme.

(a) Your ideas

_____

_____

_____

(b) Write a paragraph

[Topic   ]

Topic Sentence

Supporting Sentences

Concluding Sentence

Memo

UNIT 08
Three Tools for Learning at University

学びとは他者との関わり合いの中で生じる化学反応。自分の意見を積極的に述べよう。

Warm-Up

Exchange opinions in pairs or small groups in English. You can use the expressions, words, and phrases below.

1. How many courses are you taking this term? Which courses do you enjoy most and why?

   Ans. ....

   ....

2. What knowledge and abilities will you need to have by the time you graduate and begin working?

   Ans. ....

   ....

Useful Expressions

I'm in the faculty of… (= department, school)
My major is…
I joined this faculty because…
I'm interested in learning about…
My recent challenge is…
My best teamwork experience was in…

Useful Words and Phrases

comfort zone	in collaboration with…
communication skills	problem-solving skills
diversity	stretch zone
gain experience in…	take on a challenge
global economy	tool for learning

Pre-Reading Vocabulary Check

Match the word to its meaning.

1. anxiety
2. awkward
3. capacity
4. collaborate
5. consider
6. diverse
7. faculty
8. field
9. attain
10. involve

a. to succeed in achieving something
b. the scope or range of your ability
c. unskilled, uncomfortable, clumsy
d. allow someone to take part in something
e. an area of study, research or activity
f. various, including many different kinds
g. a feeling of worry, nervousness or stress
h. to work together on an activity or project
i. a group in a particular knowledge domain
j. to carefully think through a question or issue

1		2		3		4		5	
6		7		8		9		10	

Reading

Looking through the university's catalog you find that undergraduate* courses are of two types: general education courses and courses provided by the faculty you belong to. No matter what faculty you belong to, however, there are three fundamental* competencies you are expected to attain. They are the ability to think through complex questions, to step up to new challenges, and to work in collaboration with others. According to a 2006 report by Japan's Ministry of Economy, Trade and Industry (METI*), these are "fundamental competencies for working persons.*" Let us take a look at each in turn.

We begin with the first competency, thinking through complex questions. It's important to note here that thinking through is different from studying for. Take the university entrance exam as an example. You probably studied hard to pass the exam. How did you study for it? If you're like most students, you memorized as much information as possible: English vocabulary, historical facts, chemical formulas, mathematical equations, and so on. Knowing a lot of information enabled you to pass the entrance exam. Indeed, learning many facts has been useful in your education up to now. At university, however, it's no longer enough to simply *know the answer*. You are expected to *think through the question*. Compare the two questions below. Which must you think through?

(1) When was the first AI program developed?
(2) How can AI be used to improve our quality of life?

You probably agree that the second question is one you must think through. The two questions involve you in different mental processes. In the first, you simply remember the answer. In the second, a solution requires you to consider multiple points of information. This latter

---

undergraduate
学部の

fundamental
必須の

Ministry of Economy, Trade and Industry (METI)
経済産業省
fundamental competencies for working persons
社会人基礎力

process is what we mean by thinking through. It's a competency you gain with experience.

Why, as an undergraduate, do you need to attain this competency? This is because the world is changing rapidly. There are no easy answers to the problems we face. Climate change, child poverty, a declining birthrate, and our aging society are just a few examples. Just having a lot of knowledge is useless unless you can apply it creatively to your problem. That is why the competency to think through is a must for all undergraduates.

Let's move on to the second competency, stepping up to a challenge. Do you enjoy trying something new? If your answer is "Yes," you may already have this competency. If your answer is "No," you're not alone. Many of us shy away from a challenge. You may want to know, however, what the research has to say about it.

Studies in the field of experience-based learning* show that how you respond to a challenging situation affects your learning. If you feel comfortable, you are said to be in your comfort zone* and no growth takes place. No challenge, no learning! When you feel challenged, you are in the stretch zone.* You're exercising new mental and emotional "muscles," so to speak. You're stretching your capacity to act and think beyond what you're used to. This zone is where your growth is taking place. At other times, you may feel the situation is too challenging and you end up in the panic zone. All your energy is used up managing your anxiety with none left over for learning.

While at university, you'll encounter a variety of challenges in class and outside of class. When you find yourself facing a challenge, step up to it! Remember, each time you do so, you stretch your capacity to think and act in that situation.

Let's take a look at the third competency, the ability to work with others. If you've ever played team sports or collaborated with classmates to achieve a

experience-based learning
体験学習。実際的な活動体験を通して学ぶことを狙った学習形態。

comfort zone
居心地のいい空間

stretch zone
背伸び空間

common goal, then you have experience with this competency. In our global economy, companies in Japan and abroad seek people who are able to work well with others. Teamwork is critical to success. Furthermore, recent studies show that teams whose members have knowledge in different fields will outperform* teams whose members have knowledge in the same field. The diverse team is better at coming up with creative solutions to complex problems.

outperform
〜を凌ぐ

　　　You probably haven't decided exactly where you want to work after graduation. It's still early. The point is this: whether you go on to graduate school, work at a company, research institute, or NPO, you'll need to communicate your ideas to co-workers who may be unfamiliar with the knowledge in your field. Start now and take every opportunity to work with others so that you can develop this important skill set.

　　　By acquiring the three fundamental competencies introduced above, you can grow as a college student. Any tool requires practice in its use. You may feel awkward at first, but as you gain experience in thinking through difficult problems, stepping up to new challenges and working in collaboration with others, you'll gradually develop these tools for thinking and discover the pleasures of a university education.　　　(828 words)

チームで働く力を身につけよう！

Three Tools for Learning at University — Unit 08

True or False

Decide if each statement below is T (true) or F (false).

1. All undergraduates, regardless of their faculty, are expected to attain the same basic competencies. **T / F**
2. Your success at university depends on the amount of knowledge you already have. **T / F**
3. You are most likely to learn a new skill by staying in your comfort zone. **T / F**
4. A group whose members share the same knowledge find more creative solutions to problems. **T / F**
5. The more you practice, the more skillful you will be at using the tools of learning. **T / F**

Comprehension Questions

Answer the questions below.

1. What abilities are all undergraduates expected to attain?

2. Please look at the two questions on page 70. Why is the second question more difficult to answer than the first one?

3. Which team is better at coming up with creative solutions to complex problems, a team whose members are from different fields or a team whose members share the expertise in the same field?

Summary

 1-69

Fill in the gaps to complete the summary, then listen to the audio.

There are three (**1. f**_____) competencies all (**2. u**_____) are expected to attain. The first is (**3. t**_____) through complex questions. Rather than remembering an answer to a question, you must come up with an answer by (**4. c**_____) multiple points of information. The second competency is stepping up to a challenge. How you (**5. r**_____) to a challenge affects your learning. When you step up to a challenge, you stretch your (**6. c**_____) to think and act. The third competency is working in (**7. c**_____) with others. When you're a member of a team, you must (**8. c**_____) your ideas clearly to those who may be (**9. u**_____) with the knowledge in your field. These three competencies are (**10. t**_____) for learning you hold in your own hands.

Memo

Discussion and Writing

Think of one thing you have accomplished so far. What efforts have you made to achieve it? How did you change after the experience? Please share your ideas with your classmates and write a paragraph on this theme.

(a) Your ideas

_____

_____

_____

(b) Write a paragraph

[Topic   ]

Topic Sentence
Supporting Sentences
Concluding Sentence

UNIT 09
Laugh, and Then Think: The Ig Nobel Prize

イグ・ノーベル賞の授賞式には全身を銀色に塗った「照明係」も登場。奇抜さの演出にも余念がない。

Warm-Up

Exchange opinions in pairs or small groups in English. You can use the expressions, words, and phrases below.

1. What do you think the purpose of science is?
   Ans.

2. What is the Nobel Prize? How many Nobel Laureates do you know of?
   Ans.

Laugh, and Then Think: The Ig Nobel Prize **Unit 09**

Useful Expressions

The Nobel Prize is known for …
S/he was awarded the Nobel … Prize in …
S/he is famous for …
I first heard of her/him when …

Useful Words and Phrases

chemistry	lecture	literature	prize money
peace	speech	physics	invention
physiology	ceremony	medicine	contribution to society
economics	discovery	medal	notable pioneers
			innovative scientific technology

Pre-Reading Vocabulary Check

Match the word to its meaning.

1. parody
2. mischievous
3. friction
4. swear
5. authoritative
6. furious
7. barrage
8. assumption
9. self-indulgent
10. laureate

a. able to be trusted as being accurate or true
b. a comical imitation of something
c. the continuous firing of guns, dropping of bombs, etc.
d. the force something encounters when moving over another object
e. someone who has been given an important prize
f. something accepted as true without definite proof
g. tending to do exactly what one wants
h. naughty, teasing
i. to use rude and offensive language
j. very angry

| 1 | | 2 | | 3 | | 4 | | 5 | |
| 6 | | 7 | | 8 | | 9 | | 10 | |

77

Reading

What is the difference between the Nobel Prize and the Ig Nobel Prize? Of course they are different by two letters, and if you know the word "ignoble," you can easily hear a tone of parody in the naming: the Ig Nobel Prize may be a dishonorable version of the Nobel Prize, unworthy of attention, and nobody is likely to want it. One question remains, however: is the Ig Nobel Prize really so ignoble as the name suggests?

The Ig Nobel Prize was created in 1991 by a journal editor, Marc Abrahams, and it has since been awarded to outstanding examples of "improbable research," which is defined by Abrahams as research that "first makes people LAUGH, then makes them THINK." The winners are invited, but must travel at their own expense,* to the Ig Nobel Prize Ceremony, which is held each October at Harvard University, and receive a warm welcome from a friendly, curious, and possibly mischievous audience of 1,200. (For comparison,* the famous Nobel Banquet* held at the Stockholm City Hall is usually attended by about 1,300 people; the winners need not pay their travel expenses, I must add.) Those who attend the ceremony get the honor of* giving their acceptance speeches, but they are given just 60 seconds; if they speak longer, they must meet a cute girl called Miss Sweetie Poo, who says "Please stop. I'm bored. Please stop. I'm bored." until they finally give up.

Believe it or not,* this eccentric award reportedly attracts more than 5,000 entries each year, and just a brief look at its history seems to confirm its eccentricity. The recent winners list includes: a Medicine Prize for discovering that if you have an itch on the left side of your body, you can relieve it by looking into a mirror and scratching the right side of your body (and vice versa*); a Physics Prize for measuring the amount of friction between a shoe and a banana skin, and between a

at one's own expense
自費で、自腹で

For comparison
比較で言うと

Nobel Banquet
ノーベル賞授与式後の晩餐会

get the honor of~
〜という光栄に浴する

Believe it or not
まさかと思うだろうけども

vice versa
その逆の場合も同様に

banana skin and the floor, when a person steps on a banana skin that's on the floor; and a Peace Prize for confirming the widely held belief that swearing relieves pain.

It is not surprising that the prize has evoked mixed* responses, and it has even sparked controversy among scientists. In 1995, Sir Robert May, the chief scientific advisor to the British government, asked the organizers to stop giving Ig Nobel Prizes to any British scientists. He sent them two angry letters and also granted interviews to the press. For him the prize was an insult to "genuinely serious" science; as an authoritative gatekeeper he could not stand the sight of sheer nonsense stepping into his sacred area.

This furious voice from the British scientific establishment, however, met with unexpected reactions: he faced a barrage of criticism from his countrymen, including many scientists. In their counterarguments they pointed out that May's logic had several flaws, among which one of the most significant was concerned with the definitions of "seriousness": regardless of what assumption he had about the domain of "genuinely serious" science, most researchers of any kind engage themselves in a serious activity in their self-disciplined* and not self-indulgent ways. Indeed, if you have a chance to read the award-winning papers of the Ig Nobel Laureates, you may be amazed to find how formally and properly they describe their weird research.

If you feel uncomfortable about this apparent imbalance between style and content, remember what the Ig Nobel Prize is for: it is awarded for accomplishments which make people laugh, and then think. Thus there is nothing wrong with its having two different faces: the Ig Nobel Laureates are often serious researchers, and they may be all the funnier because of* this seriousness; their research provokes our laughter, and it may be all the more likely to arouse our thought because of this laughter.

---

mixed
賛否両論の

self-disciplined
自制心を持った、自分に厳しい

all the funnier because of~
〜だからこそ余計に可笑しい

Now let us get back to the original question: is the Ig Nobel Prize really so ignoble as the name suggests? Its
75 founder is not necessarily clear about this: "Some people covet it, others flee from it. Some see it as a hallmark of civilization, others as a scuff mark.* Some laugh with it, others laugh at it. Many praise it, a few condemn it, others are just mystified. And many people are madly in love
80 with it." Well, how is it different from the Nobel Prize?

a scuff mark
擦り傷の痕、ちょっとした恥、「脛に傷」

(732 words)

ノーベル賞メダルに刻まれたアルフレッド・ノーベル。その眼にイグ・ノーベル賞はどう映るのだろうか。

True or False

Decide if each statement below is T (true) or F (false).

1. The Ig Nobel Prize is intended as a superior version of the Nobel Prize. **T / F**
2. The Ig Nobel Laureates each year have the privilege of giving an hour-long acceptance speech without any interruption. **T / F**
3. Every year the Ig Nobel Prizes attract thousands of entries. **T / F**
4. Sir Robert May's fierce criticism of the Ig Nobel Prize was not enthusiastically welcomed by other British researchers. **T / F**
5. Marc Abrahams has always been explicit about the insignificance of the Ig Nobel Prize and is now ready to abolish it. **T / F**

Laugh, and Then Think: The Ig Nobel Prize | Unit 09

Comprehension Questions

Answer the questions below.

1. According to the Reading Passage, what are the two sources of the name "the Ig Nobel Prize"?

2. What is the role of Miss Sweetie Poo at the Ig Nobel Ceremony?

3. Why was Sir Robert May so furious with the Ig Nobel Prize?

Summary

 2-08

Fill in the gaps to complete the summary, then listen to the audio.

The Ig Nobel Prize was (**1. f**_____) in 1991 by Marc Abrahams as a unique (**2. p**_____) of the Nobel Prize. Its winners are all outstanding examples of "(**3. i**_____) research," which is defined by Abrahams as research that "first makes people LAUGH, then makes them THINK." The (**4. e**_____) of the award, on the one hand, has evoked (**5. f**_____) responses from (**6. a**_____) scientists such as Sir Robert May from Britain, who asked the organizers to stop giving Ig Nobel Prizes to any British scientists. On the other hand, however, many of his fellow scientists criticized May for his flawed (**7. a**_____) about "(**8. s**_____)": most Ig Nobel (**9. L**_____) engage themselves in research activity in self-disciplined and not (**10. s**_____) ways, and their award-winning papers often describe their weird research in an amazingly formal and proper manner.

Discussion and Writing

What is your own definition of science? Is it different from the one you find in your dictionary? If so, how is it different? Please share your ideas with your classmates and write a paragraph on this theme.

(a) Your ideas

_____

_____

_____

(b) Write a paragraph

[Topic   ]

Topic Sentence
Supporting Sentences
Concluding Sentence

Memo

UNIT 10 Ecological Thinking

セントマシュー島に置き去りにされたトナカイに何が起こったのか。真の「エコ」について考える。

Warm-Up

Exchange opinions in pairs or small groups in English. You can use the expressions, words, and phrases below.

1. What energy resources do we consume in our daily life?
   Ans.

2. What do you think we can do to save natural resources?
   Ans.

Useful Expressions

I think we should …
It is important for us to …
I hear that … is the best way to …
I don't think it is a good idea to …

Useful Words and Phrases

develop a new energy resource	reduce energy consumption
turn off the lights frequently	drive electric cars
recycling	use plastic bags
save power	

Pre-Reading Vocabulary Check

Match the word to its meaning.

1. moss	2. parallel	3. roughly	4. petroleum
5. fossilize	6. depletion	7. continent	8. isolated
9. collapse	10. emergence		

a. oil that is obtained from below the surface of the earth
b. a large piece of land surrounded by sea
c. far away from anything else
d. a person or thing that is similar to another
e. a very small green plant that grows in wet soil
f. to break down and stop functioning
g. about, not exactly
h. to be preserved in rock
i. reduction
j. the process of coming into existence

| 1 | | 2 | | 3 | | 4 | | 5 | |
| 6 | | 7 | | 8 | | 9 | | 10 | |

Reading

It was in 1944 when reindeer were first introduced to St. Matthew Island* in the Bering Sea. In those days, the island was covered with nutritious moss, which had grown for hundreds of years. The reindeer were left
5 behind after the war and they were living comfortably eating thick grass in summer and plenty of moss in winter without being attacked by any natural enemies. On this island paradise, the reindeer, having reached the age of one, gave birth to a baby every year. According to David
10 R. Klein, an American biologist who was investigating the animals at the time, the reindeer population rose from 29 in 1944 to 1,350 by 1957 and 6,000 by 1963. They died off,* however, in the next three years, eventually being reduced to a population of just 42. This happened
15 because the reindeer ate up all the grass and moss, which grew too slowly to supply enough food for the whole population. In other words, the island did not have the carrying capacity* to feed 6,000 reindeer. Furthermore, the winter of 1963–1964 was exceptionally severe in the
20 region. The reindeer barely overcame this record-breaking* climatic phenomenon. Since the 42 survivors included only one unhealthy male, it was not long before the reindeer had completely died out.

Can we see a parallel between the tragedy of St.
25 Matthew Island and an issue which we are now facing in terms of the relationship between human beings and the global environment?

Figure 1 shows the transitions of the world population from the emergence of human beings to an
30 estimate for 2100. It shows that the rate of population growth had been gradual until the 1500s, and that an exponential rise* in the world population took place after the start of the Industrial Revolution. The world population was estimated at about 1 billion around 1800.
35 At the turn of the 20th century, it was roughly 1.5 billion.

St. Matthew Island
セント・マシュー島、アラスカ州に属する島

died off
次々に死んでいく

carrying capacity
環境収容力

record-breaking
記録破りの、記録的な

exponential rise
指数的な増加（一定の時間ごとに、増加の速度が速くなる現象をさす。最初はゆっくりだが、途中から急激にふえていくようなカーブを描く）

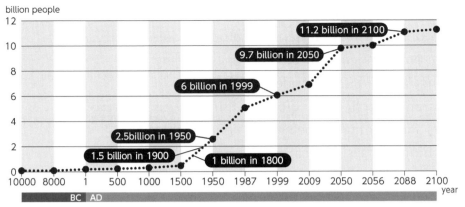

Figure 1. *Transitions of the World Population*
(Asahi Glass Foundation:Conditions for Survival [DataBook](2017)
http://www.blueplanetprize.org/databook/data001.html)

By 2000, this figure had increased to over 6 billion. The United Nations estimates that the current world population is 7.6 billion, and it will keep growing to 9.7 billion by 2050, and 11.2 billion by 2100. The problem of food supply shortages is concerning due to the rapid growth of the human population, but there are many other issues as well. Fossil fuels such as petroleum, coal, and natural gas are indispensable for human life. These are energy resources which are formed by metamorphosed* organic substances such as buried dead organisms and plants fossilized over hundreds of millions of* years. As the human economy becomes more active, the depletion of limited fossil fuels will be spurred by rapid consumption.

  Let us suppose that current human beings were the 6,000 reindeer on St. Matthew Island, and shortages of food and fossil fuels were the moss these animals consumed. We can easily predict that we will be facing severe trials in the future. If the reindeer had lived on a continent or an island that had various animals and plants coming from a nearby continent, it might have been possible to avoid their extinction or they would have died off more gradually. In a very isolated environment, however, drastic changes will happen without any means to recover from them once the circulation in the

metamorphosed
変質した

hundreds of millions of
何億もの

ecosystem collapses. The earth is a closed space. What should we do on this isolated planet to stop sudden changes in the environment and pass down life to the next generation? We need to reconsider the circulation in
65 the ecosystem and practice* "ecological thinking" in order to understand that human beings are connected to other living things in a significant way, not just by chance.* (608 words)

practice
実践する

by chance
偶然

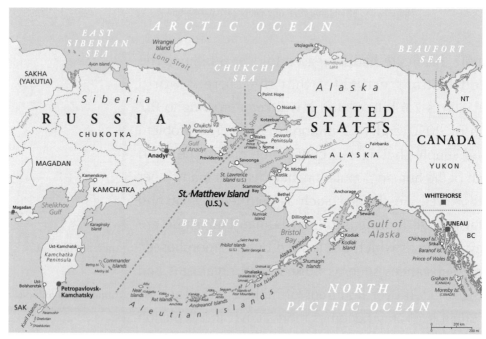

アラスカ沖ベーリング海に浮かぶセントマシュー島。

Ecological Thinking | Unit 10

True or False

Decide if each statement below is T (true) or F (false).

1. The reindeer were first introduced to St. Matthew Island before the war. **T / F**
2. One of the reasons why the reindeer could not survive was that the winter of 1963-64 was exceptionally cold. **T / F**
3. The Industrial Revolution marked the beginning of a rapid increase in world population. **T / F**
4. It is estimated that the world population will reach over 11 billion by 2100. **T / F**
5. Fossil fuels can be easily produced since humans have a scientific understanding of how they are formed. **T / F**

Comprehension Questions

Answer the questions below.

1. How many babies did the reindeer give birth to every year?

2. What are two main reasons for the extinction of the reindeer?

3. How are fossil fuels formed?

Summary

 2-13

Fill in the gaps to complete the summary, then listen to the audio.

In 1944, 29 (**1. r**_____) were first brought to St. Matthew Island. The reindeer population rose to 6,000 by 1963 because the animals had no (**2. n**_____) enemies. In 1966, however, only 42 reindeer had survived a food (**3. s**_____) and the (**4. s**_____) climate. We can see this as being similar to our problem of rapid population (**5. g**_____). The world population has been increasing (**6. d**_____) for the last two centuries, and we have been (**7. c**_____) limited (**8. f**_____) fuels. We should reconsider the earth's (**9. c**_____) capacity and think about the future of our planet more (**10. e**_____).

Discussion and Writing

Seventeen logotypes, which symbolize the 17 goals of SDGs, are shown below. Please circle the logotypes which are related to this unit. How are they related? Please share your ideas with your classmates and write a paragraph on this theme.

(https://www.un.org/sustainabledevelopment)

(a) Your ideas

_____

_____

(b) Write a paragraph

[Topic   ]

Topic Sentence

Supporting Sentences

Concluding Sentence

Memo

UNIT 11 Healthcare and Quality of Life in Two Cities

シエラレオーネ共和国の首都フリータウンの風景

Warm-Up

Exchange opinions in pairs or small groups in English. You can use the expressions, words, and phrases below.

1. If you could live as long as you wish, how many years from today would you like to live? What is essential for you to live as long as you wish?
   Ans.

2. What is happiness to you? In other words, what is essential to your happiness? How happy are you today? As a university student, what can you do today to maximize your happiness?
   Ans.

Healthcare and Quality of Life in Two Cities — Unit 11

Useful Expressions	Useful Words and Phrases
I think happiness is… I think happiness requires that …	contentment, fulfillment, health, accomplishment, peace, tranquility, challenge, love, family, friends, stability, financial security, necessities
I am feeling …	alright, pretty happy, great, a little down, stressed out
To maximize my happiness today, I can …	take a break, take care of myself, connect with my friends, go on a date, play a videogame, go shopping, read a book

Pre-Reading Vocabulary Check

Match the word to its meaning.

1. expectancy
2. vaccination
3. premature
4. complication
5. underweight
6. delivery
7. infection
8. deficiencies
9. malnutrition
10. decimate

a. a medical act to activate immunity against a disease
b. happening too early
c. a chance on average of something happening in the future
d. a condition in which one disease has been brought about by another (or other) sickness(es)
e. a condition in which a person lacks nutrients
f. conditions in which something is lacking
g. a condition in which a person's weight is considered too low
h. an act of giving birth to a baby
i. a process of disease transmission
j. to kill, destroy, or remove a large proportion of…

1		2		3		4		5	
6		7		8		9		10	

Reading

2-14～20

　　Let's go back a few decades to the year 2003. First, meet Aiko. She has just been born in Kumamoto City, Japan. When she was born, she and her mother received proper medical care from a professionally-
5 trained doctor, a midwife, and nurses, in a clean environment. Such care and comfort were quite ordinary* for her city in the year 2003.

　　Now, meet Mariam. Mariam too has just been born in 2003; she is from a city called Freetown in the
10 Republic of Sierra Leone in West Africa. When she was born, she was underweight and suffered from vitamin deficiencies. Also, her birth was not assisted by professionally-trained medical personnel. This lack of necessities and care was not unusual in her part of the
15 world.

　　Now, we are back in Japan. The year is 2009. After several healthy and active years, Aiko is now six years old and is about to enroll in primary school. By this time, she has already received vaccinations against
20 several diseases, including measles*, polio*, and diphtheria*. Around the same time in Freetown, Mariam is lucky. Why? That is because she is still alive at age six, even though a few of her close friends in the neighborhood have already passed away. There are many
25 infectious diseases*, against which not only Mariam but also her peers have not been vaccinated. Furthermore, malnutrition is widespread and has decimated the population in her part of the world.

　　In 2020, the world witnesses a coronavirus disease
30 (COVID-19) pandemic that changes people's lives. Japan and Sierra Leone are affected by the pandemic but in different magnitudes*. In Japan, the number of deaths from COVID-19 is reported to be 33,663 in August of 2022 (WHO*, 2022). Social distancing, facemasks, and
35 online classes have become essential to Aiko's life.

ordinary
普通の、通常の

measles
麻疹、はしか
polio
ポリオ、小児麻痺
diphtheria
ジフテリア

infectious disease
感染症

magnitude
規模、程度、(地震の) マグニチュード

WHO
World Health Organization
世界保健機関

Despite adversity, she still has a dream to be a medical doctor. In Sierra Leone, there are fewer cases of COVID-19 infection. There are 125 identified deaths due to COVID-19 in Sierra Leone as of March 2023 (WHO, 2023). This low mortality* could be attributed to geographical and demographic factors. In particular, Sierra Leone's geographical location which limited intercommunication of people to and from countries with high prevalence*, and the country's low population density (114 per km^2) possibly prevented the spread of the virus. However, other health risks surround Mariam and her peers in a more powerful way than the COVID-19 pandemic. A year earlier, she lost a baby during delivery. Fortunately, Mariam survived. Premature deaths are not uncommon in Sierra Leone.

Thirteen years have passed since 2020. Now, it is 2033; Aiko, now 30 years old, is a pediatrician* in Kumamoto. In the same year, she gives birth to a baby girl. During and after the labor and delivery at the hospital, Aiko and her baby are nursed with great care by medical practitioners. In Sierra Leone, Mariam too is in a hospital. However, she is there, not to give birth like Aiko, but for weakness and fatigue associated with human immunodeficiency* virus (HIV) infection, which is a common disease in her part of the world.

Back in Japan, it is 2039. Aiko—now a doctor, a wife, and a mother—is 36 years old. Like many Japanese people of her age, she undergoes a health check-up. It confirms her sound health and well-being. On average, the life expectancy* of Japanese women, such as Aiko's, is 87 years (2019, WHO estimate). Likewise, Mariam would also be 36 years of age in 2039, if she were alive. Unfortunately, she is no longer with us: she had passed away two years earlier when she was 34, as a result of complications of HIV infection, more commonly known as acquired immune deficiency syndrome (AIDS). In addition to HIV, there are many other health risks that

mortality
死亡、死亡率

prevalence
有病率、流行

pediatrician
小児科医

immunodeficiency
免疫不全

life expectancy
平均余命、平均寿命

could have killed Mariam in her part of the world. Mariam's story is not an extraordinary case in Sierra Leone.

Much of the preceding tale was created by the World Health Organization based on some facts and imagination. What do you think about the lives of the two women? Why are they so different? After reading the above narrative, what do you see in the table below? Do you think that people in your society—including yourself—take too many things for granted—that is, without appreciating their (and your) quality of life (QOL), environment, and possessions—when, in fact, the vast majority of people in many other societies, such as Sierra Leone, desperately lack daily necessities, including healthcare? If your answer to the last question is a simple "Yes" without hesitation, then it may be time you started appreciating what you have and began to apply yourself to developing your fullest potential as a university student.

(787 words)

Health-related Indicators of Japan and Sierra Leone

Indicator	Japan	Sierra Leone
Life expectancy at birth, male/female (year, 2019)	81.5/86.9	59.6/61.9
Maternal mortality ratio (per 100,000 live births, year 2017)	5	1,120
Proportion of births attended by skilled health personnel (%, years 2012-2021)	100	87

Data source: World Health Organization

True or False

Decide if each statement below is T (true) or F (false).

1. When Aiko was born, the treatment she received at the hospital was special in her city. **T / F**
2. Lack of vaccinations in her childhood was the cause of Mariam's death. **T / F**
3. It can be seen that Sierra Leone probably has not only inadequate health-related services, but also a less developed economy than that of Japan. **T / F**
4. The author probably thinks that more people in developed countries need to appreciate what they have. **T / F**
5. In both Japan and Sierra Leone, women tend to live longer than men. **T / F**

Comprehension Questions

Answer the questions below.

1. Why was Mariam lucky to be alive at age six?

2. According to the passage, why were there relatively few cases of COVID-19 in Mariam's country?

3. What caused Mariam's death?

Summary

 2-21

Fill in the gaps to complete the summary, then listen to the audio.

The narrative illustrates the (**1. c**_____) lives of two women, one in Kumamoto and the other in Freetown (**2. r**_____). Aiko was born under medical care at birth, which ensured her health, while Mariam's birth lacked such care, leaving her not only (**3. u**_____) but also with vitamin (**4. d**_____). Over time, Mariam's peers died as they fell victim to infections and (**5. m**_____), unfamiliar in Aiko's world. As a teenager, Aiko pursued education, while Mariam became a mother without any formal (**6. e**_____). By age 30, Aiko achieved success as a doctor and mother, while Mariam faced death from HIV (**7. i**_____). At the age of 34, Mariam dies of AIDS, while Aiko is (**8. e**_____) to live for many years to come. More people living in (**9. d**_____) countries such as Japan should be aware of and grateful for what they have in their lives, if they are not (**10. t**_____) already.

Note: The preceding narrative and its summary are based on the World Health Organization's visual narrative, "A Tale of Two Girls," https://www.who.int/features/2003/11/en/
License: CC BY-NC-SA 30 IGO

Memo

Discussion and Writing

In your opinion, what is necessary for happiness in life? Is health essential to happiness? How do health and happiness relate to each other? Please share your ideas with your classmates and write a paragraph on this theme.

(a) Your ideas

_____

_____

_____

(b) Write a paragraph

[Topic   ]

Topic Sentence

Supporting Sentences

Concluding Sentence

UNIT 12 Sports, Culture, and Communication

国際スポーツ大会は、文化交流や調和を促し、目標を共有することで世界の人々を結び付ける。

Warm-Up

Exchange opinions in pairs or small groups in English. You can use the expressions, words, and phrases below.

1. Do you like sports? If no, why? If yes, which sports do you like to play? Which sports do you like to watch live or on TV? Why?
   Ans.

2. How can sports help promote international communication? How can international sporting events help to improve relationships among people of diverse backgrounds?
   Ans.

Sports, Culture, and Communication | **Unit 12**

Useful Expressions

My favorite sport or sporting event is …
I think sports can bring people together because …
I am a fan of … because …
Fair play and sportsmanship is important because …

Useful Words and Phrases

game	global	culture	fair play
match	intercultural	skills	fan
points	communication	sportsmanship	Olympic athlete
runs	amateur sports	competition	Olympic medal
	professional sports		

Pre-Reading Vocabulary Check

Match the word to its meaning.

1. intercultural	2. sportsmanship	3. medal	4. amateur
5. patriotic	6. culture	7. amity	8. ambassador
9. goodwill	10. perspective		

a. fair treatment of others, especially in sports
b. the customs, arts, social institutions of a nation, people, or social group
c. taking place between cultures
d. a friendly relationship
e. having or expressing devotion to and strong support for one's country
f. a person who acts as a representative or promoter of an activity or country
g. friendly, helpful, or cooperative feelings or attitude
h. a metal disc awarded as a distinction to someone
i. a person who does something, especially a sport, without getting paid
j. a point of view

1		2		3		4		5	
6		7		8		9		10	

Reading

The *World Sports Encyclopedia* states that there are 8,000 indigenous* sports and sporting games around the world, and they are played by people of all ages and backgrounds. There are many benefits to playing sports. For example, they promote a healthy body and mind. Sports also teach people teamwork, sportsmanship, and discipline.* While international sporting events may bring out patriotic feelings in some individuals, they can also lead to amity among diverse groups of people. Whether you are a professional athlete getting paid to play a sport you love, or an amateur athlete representing your school or country at a competition, sports help people bond around a common activity. Sports can also create harmony and foster international understanding.

When we look at the ways that sports bring people together,* we can imagine how these interactions might extend to the international arena. In particular, for major amateur international sporting events such as the FIFA World Cup, the Rugby World Cup, and the Winter and Summer Olympic Games, there are many things that happen before, during, and after these events that promote greater intercultural communication.

First, each event is hosted by a particular country. When this happens, an awareness* of the host country and culture is raised. For example, in 2010, the FIFA World Cup was hosted by South Africa. This event gave South Africa a chance to showcase* the beauty of its landscape and its unique culture. It also gave the host country a chance to move beyond* its troubled history. It was an important event that led to a better understanding of African culture and also increased tourism and trade.

Second, each athlete has a passion for and love of their sport. This passion is true for all sports, for example, major sports such as baseball or basketball, or lesser-known sports such as Alpine Skiing* or Curling.* Sharing those same feelings, goals, and passion with a person from another culture, religion, and language creates friendships and goodwill that can last long after the competition is over.

Third, when people play a sport, there is an intense desire to achieve individual and team goals; however, there are rules that must be followed, and these make the playing field level.* The starting line for all athletes is equal, and with training, sweat, and great effort, everyone has a chance to succeed. Nonetheless, in some competitions there are athletes or teams that are considered to be the weaker or less-experienced competitor; they are called "underdogs". Underdogs can sometimes surprise people by performing better than expected and winning the competition. The underdog's ability to overcome challenges often inspires support from people from all around the world who cheer for them to win a game or medal.

level
対等な、公平な

Regardless of the outcome of a competition, good sportsmanship is always important. In a fair game, everyone gains something. An excellent example of good sportsmanship is the Japan Men's National Rugby Team. At the 2015 Rugby World Cup, the Japan national team played really hard and had some wonderful victories. After their wins, Japanese players showed tremendous respect and humility* towards their opponents. This behavior united people around the world and motivated them to cheer for Japan's success. This event created great interest in the sport, and continued to grow when Japan hosted the Rugby World Cup in 2019.

humility
謙虚さ

Furthermore, from a cultural perspective, much can be learned through international competition. In many cases, such as with soccer, players exchange game shirts and create nice memories of their competition with diverse peoples. Even for audiences watching the games from their home countries, people become intrigued by the events and host countries. These events give sports fans, both young and old, the opportunity to virtually visit faraway host countries such as, Brazil, China, Japan, Korea, South Africa and the United States of America. In ideal situations, politics and conflicts are paused during these games, and nations present* themselves in the best possible way. Indeed, these events are a blend of national pride and international communication as ambassadors from each country compete and celebrate each other's excellence.

    In conclusion, sports and international sporting events help people to take a break from problems in a world that is often divided by conflicts. The shared bonds that are formed among athletes and spectators remind everyone that people have more in common than we realize. This precious recognition of our shared humanity is a giant step toward global understanding.   (736 words)

present
表す、示す

スポーツを通して、言葉や国籍を超えた友情も生まれる。

True or False

Decide if each statement below is T (true) or F (false).

1. Amateur athletes receive payment for participating in sporting events.   **T / F**
2. Host countries of international sporting events hope to benefit by increasing tourism and trade.   **T / F**
3. An underdog in a sporting event is a team or player that is not expected to win.   **T / F**
4. In 2015, Japan hosted the Rugby World Cup.   **T / F**
5. A positive side of international sporting events is that past and present political conflicts are sometimes put on hold.   **T / F**

Sports, Culture, and Communication | Unit 12

Comprehension Questions

Answer the questions below.

1. What happens when a country hosts sporting events like the FIFA World Cup?

2. How can underdogs in sports competitions inspire support from people around the world?

3. How do soccer players create nice memories of their competition with diverse peoples?

Summary

 2-30

Fill in the gaps to complete the summary, then listen to the audio.

Perhaps one of the greatest benefits of international sporting events is that people from all around the world, regardless of their culture, (**1. r**_____), or language, can recognize that they can create (**2. h**_____). Athletes (**3. b**_____) around a common activity and share passion for the sport they play. In particular, major (**4. a**_____) international sporting events help promote better (**5. i**_____) communication. When each event is hosted by a (**6. p**_____) country, people want to learn more about that country and this even increases (**7. t**_____) and trade. International competitions also help people to take a break from problems or (**8. c**_____) in the world. Both athletes and spectators recognize that people have more in (**9. c**_____) than we realize and our shared (**10. h**_____) is a giant step toward global understanding.

Discussion and Writing

Do you agree with the idea that sports can promote intercultural understanding, and it actually may help lead to world peace? Please share your ideas with your classmates and write a paragraph on this theme.

(a) Your ideas

(b) Write a paragraph

[Topic   ]

Topic Sentence
Supporting Sentences
Concluding Sentence

Memo

UNIT 13 Form and Function in Classical Music

17〜18世紀のバロック時代において、室内楽、オペラ等の芸術は重要な役割を担っていた。

Warm-Up

Exchange opinions in pairs or small groups in English. You can use the expressions, words, and phrases below.

1. Why do you think people listen to music? What do you think the purpose of music is?

   Ans.
   ....
   ....

2. Discuss with a partner your favorite kind of music and how often you listen to music.

   Ans.
   ....
   ....

Form and Function in Classical Music | Unit 13

Useful Expressions

I like to listen to…
… is my favorite genre of music.
I listen to music (   ) times a week.
What kind of music do you like?

Useful Words and Phrases

J-pop	classical music	fusion
K-pop	heavy metal	folk
rock and roll	punk rock	club music
jazz	rockabilly	

Pre-Reading Vocabulary Check

Match the word/phrase to its meaning.

1. ritual
2. enhance
3. notation system
4. harmony
5. ornate
6. patron
7. legitimize
8. legacy
9. special occasion
10. pound

    a. something very highly decorated, often too much for practical use
    b. to intensify, increase, or improve the value of something
    c. to hit something heavily or repeatedly
    d. a person who offers financial support to an artist
    e. a serious and important series of actions, often used in a ceremony
    f. a combination of simultaneously sounded musical notes to produce a pleasing effect
    g. to convince people to accept a system or ruler as trustworthy or acceptable
    h. a system of writing musical notes down on paper
    i. an important day or event
    j. the way that people remember you after you die

1		2		3		4		5	
6		7		8		9		10	

Reading

　　Most people enjoy listening to music, but have you ever thought about the purpose of music? Throughout human history, music has been an important form of artistic expression for entertainment and in ceremonies
5 and rituals. Flutes made from elephant tusks* and the bones of birds have been found that were more than 40,000 years old. However, while music has long been used to enhance or emphasize the expression of human emotions, it has also served a very practical function that
10 reflected the historical circumstances of the time. Let's look at some examples.

　　It may be surprising to learn that Christianity most strongly contributed to the development of Western music as we know it. From around 500 AD, Christian monks
15 chanted* passages from the Bible to help their followers* remember them. But after the development of a musical notation system in the 11th century AD, the study of music as an art form became much more widespread, and musical compositions rapidly evolved in terms of rhythm,
20 coordination among instruments, and especially in the development of harmony. Over the following centuries, composers began to create increasingly* complex songs for many new combinations of voices and instruments, and to serve a wide variety of functions.

25　　The Baroque Period* (1600-1750AD) produced some of the most complex music in human history. The word "baroque" comes from Portuguese, meaning "irregular* pearl," which refers to how art and music during that period, while beautiful, were thought to be
30 too ornate for practical use. Probably the most important patron of the arts during the Baroque Period was France's King Louis XIV (1638 -1715AD), who had complete control over every decision made about France, from the size of the French army, to laws, taxes, and especially
35 how much money to spend on the development of art and

elephant tusks
象牙

chant
歌う、詠唱する
followers
弟子たち

increasingly
ますます

The Baroque Period
バロック時代

irregular
歪んだ

music. But Louis didn't just support art and music because he loved it, he did so as a way of legitimizing his power. He constantly surrounded himself with beautiful architecture, paintings, and music because he wanted the people of France to believe that he was chosen by God as their ruler, and he believed that it would preserve his legacy as one of the greatest kings in history (he was right!). As you can see, the beautiful art and music that is created for people to enjoy also serves a functional purpose that reflects the demands of history.

The head composer for King Louis was his childhood friend and dancing partner, Jean Baptiste Lully.* Lully composed many different kinds of music based on the needs of Louis's court*. King Louis often attended church services in the morning, so Lully had to compose many songs for singers, organ, and a few instruments, to be played in the royal chapel. In the evenings, King Louis often held small parties, so Lully had to compose chamber music* for dancing or just to have in the background, which was usually performed by a small group of stringed instruments, harpsichord, and some flutes. But King Louis also needed music for outdoor events such as when he went hunting or when parading his army. So Lully composed music for drums, trumpets, and other horned instruments that could be played loudly enough to be heard outdoors.

Finally, Lully needed to compose music for large concerts such as operas or ballets on special occasions, so he united all of the instruments; woodwinds*, brass, strings, and drums, to form an orchestra. Actually, keeping so many musicians playing together at the same time was very difficult, so Lully used to pound a large staff* on the ground to help them play together in time. One time when he was conducting an opera, Lully accidentally pounded the staff onto his foot, which became so badly damaged that he eventually died from it. Much of the music that we now know today came from composers

Jean Baptiste Lully
ジャン＝バティスト・リュリ（1632-87）ルイ14世の時代に活躍した作曲家
court
宮廷

chamber music
室内楽

woodwinds
木管楽器

staff
こん棒

like Lully, who helped meet the demands of history in their compositions.

The development of music in history can give us important clues about how musical form is influenced by the function for which it is used. Modern singers, for example, are often accompanied by* simple instrumental music so that it is easy to understand the lyrics. On the other hand, fast instrumental music with a strong beat is much easier to dance to. So the next time you listen to your favorite song, think about the function that it was made for. It may help you enjoy it even more!

(743 words)

accompanied by
伴奏される

ジャン＝バティスト・リュリ

True or False

Decide if each statement below is T (true) or F (false).

1. Christian monks used to sing Bible passages to help their followers remember them.　　　　　　　　　　　　　　　　　　　　　T / F
2. Musical composition advanced very quickly after a system for writing music down on paper was developed.　　　　　　　　　　　T / F
3. The word "baroque" refers to the simple quality of music during the period.　　　　　　　　　　　　　　　　　　　　　　　　T / F
4. One reason why Louis supported art and music was to get French citizens to recognize his power over them.　　　　　　　　　　T / F
5. Lully composed many different kinds of music based on the needs of King Louis.　　　　　　　　　　　　　　　　　　　　　　T / F

Comprehension Questions

Answer the questions below.

1. Why did Christian monks chant passages from the Bible?

2. What were the two reasons why King Louis was such a strong patron of the arts?

3. What instruments were typically used for outdoor events?

Summary

 2-37

Fill in the gaps to complete the summary, then listen to the audio.

Music has been used (**1.** t_____) history to enhance the (**2.** e_____) of emotions. However, it also served a functional purpose that (**3.** r_____) what was happening in history. The Baroque Period was when the most (**4.** c_____) and (**5.** o_____) music was composed, because Louis XIV surrounded himself with art and music to (**6.** l_____) his power as King of France. Jean Baptiste Lully (**7.** c_____) many different kinds of music to serve King Louis during his rule. Many of the combinations of instruments and musical forms that Lully (**8.** d_____) during the Baroque Period are still being used today. Understanding how music was used in (**9.** h_____) can provide us with important clues on how form is influenced by (**10.** f_____).

Discussion and Writing

What genre of music has had the largest impact on society over the last 50 years? Why do you think so? Please share your ideas with your classmates and write a paragraph on this theme.

(a) Your ideas

_____

_____

_____

(b) Write a paragraph

[Topic   ]

Topic Sentence
Supporting Sentences
Concluding Sentence

Memo

UNIT 14 Looking at Art of Other Cultures

Figure 1 Dancing Ganesha,
10th century, India
(www.metmuseum.org)

ヒンドゥー教の神、ガネーシャ。シヴァの息子で象の頭部が特徴的。4本の腕を持つ姿で表されることが多い。現世利益をもたらすとされる。

Figure 2 Standing Bodhisattva Maitreya,
3rd century, Pakistan
(www.metmuseum.org)

ガンダーラ仏、古代の仏教彫刻の一例。ボーディサットヴァは「菩薩（ぼさつ）」の意で、マイトレーヤは日本でいうところの弥勒菩薩。顔や衣服の表現に古代ギリシャ彫刻に似た特徴がある。

Warm-Up

Exchange opinions in pairs or small groups in English. You can use the expressions, words, and phrases below.

1. Look at the above two photos. What do you think about these figures? Which do you prefer? Why?

   Ans.
   ....
   ....

2. Look at the two figures again. Which figure do you think more people in Japan would prefer? Why?

   Ans.
   ....
   ....

Looking at Art of Other Cultures — Unit 14

Useful Expressions

I think Dancing Ganesha is…
I prefer Dancing Ganesha to Standing Bodhisattva Maitreya because…
I like both of them because…
I don't like either of them because…

Useful Words and Phrases

beautiful	ugly
scary usual	impressive
terrifying	exotic
grotesque	shocking
scary but cute	handsome
freaky but	amazing
cute	

Pre-Reading Vocabulary Check

Match the word to its meaning.

1. impartially	2. disputed	3. deity	4. apocalyptic
5. BCE	6. dharma chakra	7. CE	8. refute
9. curator	10. sophisticated		

a. highly developed and complicated
b. to prove that (someone) is wrong
c. of the biblical Apocalypse
d. fairly, without biases and beliefs
e. a keeper or custodian of a museum
f. Common Era, the period since the birth of Christ when the Christian calender starts counting years
g. subject to debate and argument
h. Before Common Era
i. the wheel of the law
j. a god or goddess

1		2		3		4		5	
6		7		8		9		10	

Reading

In your new life as a college student, you may find time to visit museums and galleries. Looking at art from other cultures will stimulate your curiosity. You might try to understand a culture through its artistic creations. In
5 such attempts, however, your religious, cultural, and political beliefs could influence your perceptions and prevent you from evaluating foreign art impartially. In the history of art, unfortunately, we have often experienced misunderstandings because of our biases. Some of the
10 most disputed art in this sense is found in South Asia.

One example is Indian statues of Ganesha.* This Hindu deity has multiple arms and an elephant head. Today, we know these features have sophisticated religious significance in Hindu traditions. However, to
15 medieval and early modern European Christians, the statues were nothing but scary monsters. European travel accounts from these periods depicted Indian people worshiping monsters from the Greco-Roman* classics or devils from the apocalyptic literature.* According to South
20 Asian art historian Partha Mitter,* these monsters are products of the Europeans' fear of the unfamiliar. This misunderstanding persisted in the European imagination throughout the medieval period and well into the 18th century.

25 In the 19th century, however, the art of South Asia suddenly attracted enthusiastic European scholars, when British colonial officials "discovered" something familiar to them – ancient Buddhist sculptures with Greek-style elements – in northwestern India, then called Gandhara*
30 (part of Afghanistan and Pakistan today). Studying these objects, Alfred Foucher,* an early French Orientalist,* claimed that they had been created in Greek colonies in Bactria after Alexander the Great's invasion of India in the fourth century BCE. In ancient Buddhist narratives, the
35 Buddha figure was usually absent, represented instead in

Ganesha
ガネーシャ（ヒンドゥー教の神）象の頭部を持っている。願いをかなえてくれると信じられており、インドで広く信仰されている。Figure 1 を参照。

Greco-Roman
古代ギリシャ・ローマの
the apocalyptic literature
ここではキリスト教の「ヨハネの黙示録」を指す。
Partha Mitter
パーサー・ミッター（1938－　）。インド美術研究者。

Gandhara
ガンダーラでは1世紀ごろから仏教文化が栄え、多くの仏像が制作された。これ以前は、仏陀は人間の形ではなく、象徴的にだけ表現されていたため（法輪や足跡など）、仏像は作られなかった。そのため、ガンダーラは仏像発祥の地の一つとされている。
Alfred Foucher
アルフレッド・フーシェ（1865－1952）
Orientalist
オリエント（ヨーロッパから見て東に位置する世界・東洋）を研究する人を指す。しかし今日ではオリエントという語が差別的だと考える人もあり、あまり使われない。

the form of his symbols, such as his footprints and the dharma chakra. Then in the first century CE, images of the Buddha in human form, resembling Greek sculpture, began emerging from the Gandhara region. Foucher, and many other European scholars, interpreted this phenomenon to mean that the ancient Greeks or their descendants* had "taught" South Asians how to create images of the sacred in human figures. Thus, Gandhara, they assumed, provided proof of the Greco-Roman origin of Buddha figures.

At the end of the 19th century, however, South Asian art historians began to question this Eurocentric view, using their philological expertise* and local resources. Was South Asian art valuable only when it was affected by Western cultures? Pioneer Indian archaeologist and art historian Rájendralála Mitra* challenged the assumption that a Greek artist in a Greek colony had been responsible for creating the first Buddha statue. Mitra, who was also a political leader fighting for Indian independence, emphasized the glorious past of Indian art rather than brief foreign influence. He used his knowledge of ancient texts to refute the European scholars.

Following Mitra, and in line with the rise of Indian nationalism in the early 20th century, more South Asian intellectuals denied the superiority of European civilizations. One of the most published scholars in this group was Ananda Coomaraswamy,* born in Ceylon (Sri Lanka today) and educated in England. Although he recognized some degree of Greek influence on the Gandhara Buddhist sculptures, he believed that the Gandhara style was just a variant of the regional art of the time. Instead, he placed the authentic origin of Buddha images in Mathura* (in northern India), where sculpture had fewer Greek elements. In this strategic move, Coomaraswamy claimed that the origin of the Buddha image was Indian, not foreign. Later, as a curator of the Museum of Fine Arts, Boston, he widely published

---

descendant
子孫

philological expertise
文献学の専門知識

Rájendralála Mitra
ラジェンドララーラ・ミトラ (1822–1891)。イギリス人が創設した研究所 Asiatic Society で、インド人初の同所の会長となった。

Ananda Coomaraswamy
アーナンダ・クーマラスワミ (1877–1947)。インドの芸術・哲学の研究者で、ボストン美術館の東洋美術学芸員。

Mathura
マトゥラーはガンダーラとほぼ同時期に仏像が多く作られた地方。ガンダーラの仏像がギリシャ的であるのに対し、マトゥラーの仏像はよりインド的と言われている。どちらが仏像誕生の地かは論争が続いている。

influential books on the philosophy and art of South Asia and helped Westerners understand the cultural background of Indian art.

However, these arguments, pregnant with political motives, have given way to new generations of scholars from various parts of the post-colonial world today. They seek alternative methods of studying non-Western art in less biased ways and with respect toward the unfamiliar.

Our curiosity will certainly help us understand the diverse cultures of the world, but we should always be aware of our own prejudices when we look at the art of other cultures. (680 words)

悪魔の像に礼拝するインド人。15世紀イタリア人 Ludovico di Varthema による旅行記がドイツで翻訳出版（1515年）されたときに添えられた挿絵。旅行記の記述をもとに挿絵画家の想像で描かれた。(Courtesy of the John Carter Brown Library)

True or False

Decide if each statement below is T (true) or F (false).

1. In early European travel accounts, sacred statues of Hindu deities with multiple arms and animal heads are described as divine beings. **T / F**
2. In the early 20th century, European scholars became interested in the art of South Asia. **T / F**
3. In the 19th century, ancient Buddhist sculptures with Greek-style elements were found in Gandhara. **T / F**
4. Foucher claimed ancient Buddhist sculptures with Greek-style elements had been created in Greece and taken to Gandhara. **T / F**
5. Mitra thought the genuine origin of Buddha images in South Asia was in Mathura, where sculptures had fewer Greek elements. **T / F**

Comprehension Questions

Answer the questions below.

1. How did Europeans depict Hindu deities?

2. Why did ancient Buddhist sculptures in Gandhara attract European scholars?

3. Why did Coomaraswamy claim that Mathura, not Gandhara, was the origin of Buddha sculptures?

Summary

 2-45

Fill in the gaps to complete the summary, then listen to the audio.

Our beliefs often prevent us from (1. e_____) arts of other cultures (2. i_____). For example, Hindu (3. d_____) were depicted as (4. s_____) monsters in Europe. When ancient Buddhist (5. s_____) with Greek-style elements were found in (6. n_____) India, European scholars claimed that those sculptures had been created in Greek colonies after Alexander the Great's (7. i_____) of India. They thought that the ancient Greeks or their (8. d_____) had taught South Asians how to create those sculptures. Mitra, an Indian art historian, used his knowledge of ancient texts to (9. r_____) the European scholars. In evaluating other cultures, we should understand our own (10. p_____).

Discussion and Writing

Search for the word "Japonisme" on the Internet. Find a foreign artist who was influenced by Japanese art and choose one work of art by the artist. In which part of the work do you see influence? Why do you think the artist adopted Japanese art in his/her work? Please share your ideas with your classmates and write a paragraph on this theme.

(a) Your ideas

_____

_____

_____

(b) Write a paragraph

[Topic   ]

Topic Sentence
Supporting Sentences
Concluding Sentence

Memo

UNIT 15
Interdisciplinary Studies: Where Science and Humanities Meet

大学とは、様々なバックグラウンドを持った人と出会い、交流できる場である。

Warm-Up

Exchange opinions in pairs or small groups in English. You can use the expressions, words, and phrases below.

1. What course do you like the best at university? Why?
   Ans.
   ....
   ....

2. Are you a humanities major or a science major? Was it difficult for you to decide which course to take?
   Ans.
   ....
   ....

Interdisciplinary Studies: Where Science and Humanities Meet **Unit 15**

Useful Expressions

I'm a … major.
It was pretty … to decide because I wanted to become …
My favourite subject was …, so …
I wasn't very sure what I wanted to study, but …

Useful Words and Phrases

humanities	Japanese geography
science	biology
easy	physics
difficult	be interested in …
a psychologist	had no choice
an engineer	my parents recommended …

Pre-Reading Vocabulary Check

Match the word to its meaning.

1. aptitude	2. integrate	3. feasible	4. grasp
5. symptom	6. deprive	7. psychiatrist	8. discrepancy
9. hectic	10. appreciation		

- a. to completely understand
- b. to prevent someone from having something
- c. a doctor who treats mental illnesses
- d. very busy
- e. natural ability or skill
- f. a difference between two things
- g. to combine, put together
- h. visible sign of illness
- i. possible
- j. recognition and enjoyment of the good qualities of someone or something

1		2		3		4		5	
6		7		8		9		10	

Reading

  Thinking of which university to enter, you must have made one of the most important decisions for your academic future: whether you go to the humanities course (*bunkei*) or the science course (*rikei*). Probably you were
5 asking yourself which courses you had the aptitude for, considering your proficiencies* in the major subjects, such as math, Japanese, English, etc. Many faculties and departments in universities are divided into these two courses, and you must have intensively studied some
10 selected subjects for your entrance exams. Generally speaking, those who are strong in math and physics are encouraged to go to science courses, and those whose favorite subjects include arts, languages, and history are more likely to find suitable courses in humanities. In fact,
15 the curriculum for science courses includes math and physics as major subjects, and that for the humanities has literature, philosophy, and language studies. So, are humanities useless for science students? Is studying science a waste of time for humanities students?

20   Whichever course you are taking now, both science and humanities are essential. In fact, the barriers between science and humanities have been lowered, and some universities even have departments and courses where humanities and science are integrated. Look at
25 environmental study. With the aim of* protecting the earth from a variety of threats such as pollution and global warming, study of the environment consists of the appreciation of the environment and research on methods to protect it. The former is fostered through humanities,
30 and classes such as arts and literature are good exercises in which the concept of beauty is pursued. Through these lessons, you learn to be sensitive to beauty in nature, which is the basis for developing an environmentally friendly mindset. On the other hand, the study of science
35 is essential to find practical and feasible methods for

proficiencies
力量

With the aim of
〜の目的で

saving the natural environment. Moreover, many environmental problems are also global issues and cannot be solved without international cooperation. Thus, a good command* of foreign languages and communication is important as well.

The integration of science and humanities can also be found in the field of medicine: narrative* medicine or narrative-based medicine (NBM) has recently been attracting attention from both doctors and patients. As the name suggests, this is an interdisciplinary* field where literature (narrative) and science (medicine) work together. In NBM, doctors and patients build up healthy human relationships through dialogue. However, their interaction means more than that. By paying attention to the stories told by patients, doctors try to grasp all the problems surrounding the patients, not only those related to their illnesses but also those affecting their whole lives. This is because the cause of the patients' suffering cannot be identified from symptoms alone, and their narratives may offer some clues that lead to recovery. Moreover, in choosing the best therapy, doctors should take into account the patients' lifestyle or reasons for living. By considering and analyzing the problems comprehensively,* doctors and patients may find a treatment satisfactory for both. However, finding the best treatment is not the goal of narrative medicine; some doctors believe that the act of narrative itself can lead to healing.

Because of the dramatic progress in science, medical services began to regard evidence (that is, facts and findings) as objective and reliable, neglecting a patient's voice as subjective and groundless.* However, not even the best treatment from the viewpoint of science always brings satisfaction to patients, and this often deprives doctors of a sense of accomplishment. Distinguishing the patient's experience of illness and the doctor's attention to disease, Arthur Kleinman,* a psychiatrist at Harvard Medical School, argues that the former, an area of the humanities, tends to be neglected in the field of medicine, while the latter, based on scientific evidence, is considered to be what medicine should be. Many doctors like Kleinman worry that this discrepancy is the root of many problems in medicine.

  The environment and medicine are not exceptions, and there are many other fields of study in which both science and humanities are combined to address* a variety of problems. The university is a place where you can acquire a broad knowledge of different fields while pursuing your own research topic. You might disagree, saying, "My life is hectic. How could I find time to worry about what other people are studying?" Even so, you should at least be interested in what is happening in other fields of study and interact with teachers and friends working in different areas. Reading extensively may also help you in this regard. When you get stuck in your major and have difficulties finding solutions, it may be the courage to look at your neighbors that opens up a way forward.

(779 words)

address 解決する

様々なコミュニケーションが行き交う医療の現場は、まさにサイエンスとヒューマニティの融合である。

参考文献の紹介

ナラティブ・メディスンは、物語能力に着目した医療・医学教育のことで、AI 等科学技術の飛躍的進化の一方で軽視されがちな人間性を重視した医療分野です。本分野についてより知るために、『ナラティブ・メディスンの原理と実践』(リタ・シャロン他著、斎藤 清二・栗原 幸江・斎藤章太郎訳) をお薦めします。そこには、ナラティブ・メディスンの基本的理念と実践方法がわかりやすく説明されています。

True or False

Decide if each statement below is T (true) or F (false).

1. Some universities have courses where humanities and science are integrated.
   T / F
2. International cooperation is essential when solving environmental problems.
   T / F
3. In NBM, the doctors must choose the best therapy by listening carefully to the stories told by the patients.
   T / F
4. Nowadays, many doctors believe that the humanities are obstacles to their jobs.
   T / F
5. The best way to succeed in your major is to just stick to your own research field.
   T / F

Comprehension Questions

Answer the questions below.

1. How do university students learn to be sensitive to beauty in nature?

2. What should doctors take into account in choosing the best therapy?

3. What often deprives doctors of a sense of accomplishment?

Summary

Fill in the gaps to complete the summary, then listen to the audio.

Many (**1. f**_____) and departments in universities are divided between two fields, humanities and science. However, the (**2. b**_____) between them have been (**3. l**_____) and some universities even have departments and courses where humanities and science are (**4. i**_____). The study of the environment is an example of the integration of science and humanities. Narrative-based medicine is another example, where doctors and patients build up healthy (**5. r**_____) through (**6. d**_____). The patients' experience of (**7. i**_____) should not be (**8. n**_____), because it may lead to their (**9. r**_____). Knowing what is happening in other fields of study is a good way for university students to (**10. a**_____) broad knowledge.

Memo

Interdisciplinary Studies: Where Science and Humanities Meet | Unit 15

Discussion and Writing

Do some research on narrative medicine/narrative-based medicine on the Internet and discuss the role of literature in medical education. Do you agree that doctors should read literature? How about scientists, engineers, or business persons? Please share your ideas with your classmates and write a paragraph on this theme.

(a) Your ideas

_____

_____

_____

(b) Write a paragraph

[Topic   ]

Topic Sentence
Supporting Sentences
Concluding Sentence

参考資料（1）

Brainstorming : (mind mapping) 英語でも日本語でも OK. アイディアを沢山書き出し、それらの関係を線で結びます。

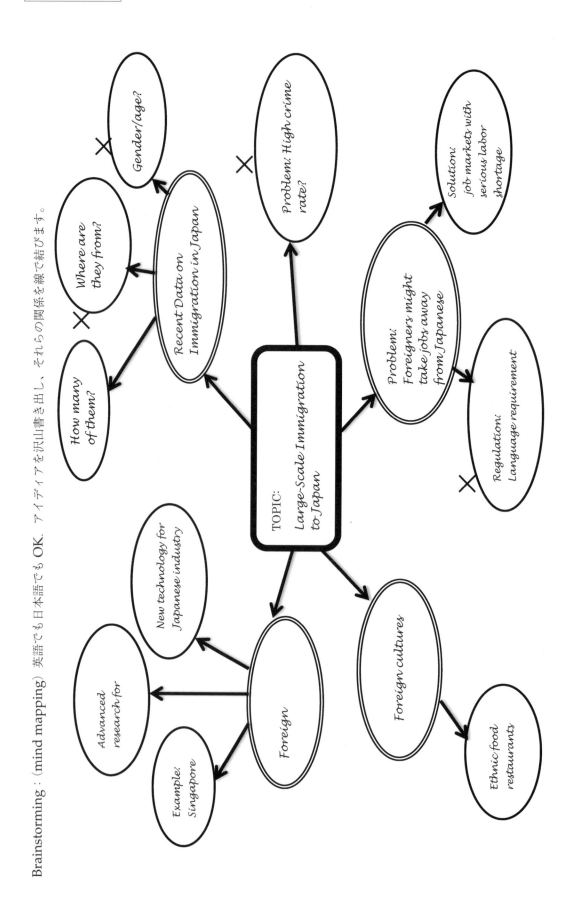

参考資料（2）

01234567 Taro Oka
May 1, 20●●
English Writing 1

Outline: Large-Scale Immigration to Japan

I. Introduction
   A. The Prime Minister's announcement of the possibility to accept large-scale immigrants and the controversy it caused
   B. Facts on foreign residents in Japan
      1. Total number
      2. Acceptance ranking in the world
   C. <u>Thesis Statement: This essay will discuss Japan's need to consider immigration, examining its potential to advance technology, provide valuable human capital, and celebrate diverse cultures.</u>

II. Positive effects of immigration (1): Immigrants could bring new technology and skills for Japanese industries
   A. Highly skilled and educated foreigners in manufacturing and technology
   B. Example: foreign researchers invited by the government of Singapore
   C. New opportunities in education in Japan

III. Positive effects of immigration (2): Immigrants could supply human capital to Japanese economy
   A. Objection to immigration: the possible job insecurity
   B. Answer to the objection: foreign workers for understaffed workplaces

IV. Positive effects of immigration (3): Japanese people could experience diverse cultures
   A. Foreign workers bring their cultures
   B. Japanese people have more opportunities to learn foreign cultures
   C. Example: foreign food restaurants

V. Conclusion

参考資料 (3)

01234567 Taro Oka
May 1, 20●●
English Writing 1

The Large-Scale Immigration to Japan

In 2018, Prime Minister Shinzo Abe announced a plan to accept up to 200,000 immigrants annually to address Japan's aging and shrinking population. By 2011, there were 2 million foreigners in Japan, making up 1.6% of the population (Hoffman, 2012). While the number of immigrants in Japan is on the rise, it ranks only 125th globally. This announcement triggered a national debate on the pros and cons of large-scale immigration. Some are against it due to concerns about productivity and wage levels. This essay will discuss Japan's need to consider immigration, examining its potential to advance technology, provide valuable human capital, and celebrate diverse cultures.

Large-scale immigration will have a significant positive impact on the manufacturing and technology sectors. Foreign labour inflows bring in an abundance of highly skilled and educated foreign workers, enriching these sectors with fresh talent and perspectives. In Singapore, researchers are invited from all over the world and funded by the government to undertake research that not only benefits the nation but also contributes to the wellbeing of the people. These researchers are at the front of advanced research and are tackling complex challenges, such as finding a cure for cancer. In Singapore's environment of collaborative innovation, where large-scale immigration is one of the factors stimulating economic growth and technological progress, the changing power of diversity is being realized in these important areas. In Japan, too, the technological advances brought about by such immigration can be expected.

Secondly, the implementation of large-scale immigration serves as a vital solution to address workforce shortages and increase Japan's human capital, thereby contributing significantly to the country's economic growth. Despite concerns about potential increases in unemployment and reduced job opportunities for local Japanese, it is crucial to recognize that certain sectors, like agriculture and nursing, consistently face understaffing issues. In such cases, the recruitment of foreign workers becomes indispensable for Japan, particularly as the nation deals with an aging population. This approach ensures the continuity of these essential services and enhances Japan's competitive position in the global market.

Thirdly, large-scale immigration provides abundant opportunities for Japanese people to experience foreign cultures, fostering an appreciation of both cultural similarities and differences that shape our global community. With a surge in immigrants, Japan can expect an expansion of restaurants offering diverse cuisines with unique taste from all over the world, enriching the culinary landscape. Japanese individuals will have the chance to engage with various facets of foreign cultures without leaving their homeland. This exposure serves as a bridge, enhancing cross-cultural understanding and creating a more interconnected, culturally enriched society, thus promoting the acceptance of diversity.

All in all, there are many upsides about introducing the large-scale immigrants to Japan. By accepting many immigrants, Japanese technology will be advanced, understaffed jobs will be filled, and diverse cultures will become more familiar to local people.

Reference

Hoffman, M. (2012, October 21). Only immigrants can save Japan. *The Japan Times*. Retrieved from http://www.japantimes.co.jp

TEXT PRODUCTION STAFF

edited by Hiroko Nakazawa	編集 中澤　ひろ子
English-language editing by Bill Benfield	英文校閲 ビル・ベンフィールド
cover design by Nobuyoshi Fujino	表紙デザイン 藤野　伸芳
text design by Hiroyuki Kinouchi (ALIUS)	本文デザイン 木野内　宏行（アリウス）

CD PRODUCTION STAFF

narrated by Howard Colefield (AmE) Jennifer Okano (AmE)	吹き込み者 ハワード・コールフィールド（アメリカ英語） ジェニファー・オカノ（アメリカ英語）

Exploring Liberal Arts in the 21st Century
21世紀の国際教養

2025年1月20日　初版発行
2025年2月15日　第2刷発行

著　者　　Japan Association of International Liberal Arts
　　　　　日本国際教養学会
発行者　　佐野　英一郎
発行所　　株式会社 成美堂
　　　　　〒101-0052　東京都千代田区神田小川町3-22
　　　　　TEL 03-3291-2261　FAX 03-3293-5490
　　　　　https://www.seibido.co.jp

印刷・製本　　倉敷印刷（株）

ISBN 978-4-7919-7318-7　　　　　　　　　　　　Printed in Japan

・落丁・乱丁本はお取り替えします。
・本書の無断複写は、著作権上の例外を除き著作権侵害となります。